TEACHING RESPONSIBILITY THROUGH PHYSICAL ACTIVITY

SECOND EDITION

Don Hellison, PhD

University of Illinois at Chicago

Human Kinetics

Library of Congress Cataloging-in-Publication Data

Hellison, Donald R., 1938–
    Teaching responsibility through physical activity / Don Hellison.--
2nd ed.
        p. cm.
Includes bibliographical references and index.
    ISBN 0-7360-4601-1 (Soft Cover)
    1. Physical education and training--Sociological aspects--Study and
teaching.   2. Responsibility--Study and teaching.   I. Title.
    GV342.27 .H45 2003
    306.4'83--dc21

                                                        2002152863

ISBN-10: 0-7360-4601-1
ISBN-13: 978-0-7360-4601-5

Acquisitions Editor: Bonnie Pettifor; **Managing Editor:** Amy Stahl; **Assistant Editor:** Derek Campbell; **Copyeditor:** Bob Replinger; **Proofreader:** Red Inc.; **Indexer:** Marie Rizzo; **Permission Manager:** Dalene Reeder; **Graphic Designer:** Andrew Tietz; **Graphic Artist:** Kathleen Boudreau-Fuoss; **Cover Designer:** Jack W. Davis; **Art Manager:** Kelly Hendren; **Illustrator:** Kathleen Boudreau-Fuoss; **Printer:** United Graphics

Printed in the United States of America
10 9 8 7 6 5 4

Human Kinetics
Web site: www.HumanKinetics.com

United States: Human Kinetics
P.O. Box 5076, Champaign, IL 61825-5076
800-747-4457
e-mail: humank@hkusa.com

Canada: Human Kinetics
475 Devonshire Road Unit 100, Windsor,
ON N8Y 2L5
800-465-7301 (in Canada only)
e-mail: orders@hkcanada.com

Europe: Human Kinetics
107 Bradford Road, Stanningley, Leeds
LS28 6AT, United Kingdom
+44 (0) 113 255 5665
e-mail: hk@hkeurope.com

Australia: Human Kinetics
57A Price Avenue, Lower Mitcham
South Australia 5062
08 8372 0999
e-mail: info@hkaustralia.com

New Zealand: Human Kinetics
Division of Sports Distributors NZ Ltd.
P.O. Box 300 226 Albany
North Shore City, Auckland
0064 9 448 1207
e-mail: info@humankinetics.co.nz

Contents

Part III   Implementation

Foreword

I have known about Don Hellison's ideas and his work with kids since the early 1970s with the publication of his *Humanistic Physical Education* (1973). In the same year I published a chapter entitled "The Humanistic Education Movement: Some Questions." When Don published *Beyond Balls and Bats,* I got the first real understanding of how his potent ideas looked in action. In the late 1970s he and I debated "Humanism Versus Behaviorism" before a packed house at AAHPERD's national convention. It was our first face-to-face meeting, and we both learned more about each other's positions and came away with what, in retrospect, was the beginning of a strong professional relationship that would also become a personal friendship that we both value. At that California AAHPERD debate we also learned that we had played high school baseball against each other in the Chicago suburbs in 1955 (yes, it's true, we are that old!).

We then twice more did our "debate show" at AAPHERD conventions in Atlanta and Portland. In each of those presentations it was clear that our positions, which looked so diametrically opposite in the mid-1970s, had important commonalities. Don found that if you work with kids in the real world, you have to have methods to get some control over their behavior and gradually work with them toward self-control and responsibility. I found that when you set up behavioral programs for kids, you have to understand that they are kids and have lives and hopes and dreams and problems. The technical stuff, while incredibly important, is not the entire tale.

Don Hellison has never wavered from the path that led him to a career in physical education working with at-risk youth. His persistence and consistency are exemplars to anybody who wants to make a contribution over time. Where he is now with his TPSR (taking personal and social responsibility) is a long way from where he was when he started, but the evolution of his approach is clear. How it evolved was the result of two key aspects of Don's work and his sense of himself and his role. He continues to read widely in youth development and other areas so that he continues to be what he has always been about—ideas! He has tested his model, replicated it if you will, in different settings and has always let it evolve to meet the needs of the kids with whom he was working in those settings. These replications have enabled him to fine-tune his approach and have made it more broadly accessible to professionals in diverse settings.

This interplay between ideas and practice is where he has most influenced my work. Don's work is solidly grounded in an important and relevant literature about youth development. Don has also taught me the value of perseverance along a path. He has helped me and others understand how important it is to be led by your experiences working with kids. I have also been profoundly influenced by his unambiguous commitment to the world of practice.

So, here we are with a new edition of this book—a book specifically devoted to helping physical education teachers understand his approach to responsibility (ideas) and implement his model successfully (practice). This is indeed a real revision, and it promises to extend his work in a place where most children and youth are found—in the schools. The ideas he presents in this revision are extraordinarily relevant to the problems physical education teachers encounter every day in their gymnasiums and on their playing fields. The strategies he lays out and the many helpful techniques he has for implementing those strategies will enable teachers to create more hospitable learning spaces, a sense of community among class members, and kids who have a better chance to grow up successfully.

Daryl Siedentop

Preface to the Second Edition

If you want to write about the truth you must write about your-self. I am the only truth I know.—Jean Rhys

This book is the latest version of my career-long effort to use sport and exercise as a vehicle for helping kids take more responsibility for their well-being and be more sensitive and responsive to the well-being of others. It summarizes the ideas and insights I have gained from working with kids and interacting with other teachers and youth workers.

In the last edition, I stated that my part-time teaching experiences with underserved youth for over two decades, along with the experiences of teachers and other professionals who have worked in more traditional settings, have provided the basis for the ideas in this book. That's still true, but now I've been at it for over three decades. That means that I have updated and modified this edition in a number of ways. Most important, I wrote this edition for PE teachers in schools. I decided to do this primarily because of the interest in the first edition shown by public school teachers and because the book *Youth Development and Physical Activity* (Hellison, Cutforth, Kallusky, Martinek, Parker, and Stiehl 2000) primarily focuses on extended-day youth work. This edition enables me to address problems common to most teachers who are interested in integrating personal and social responsibility into their practice, such as large class size, the current test-score mania (this too shall pass), what John Goodlad called the "deep culture" of schools, and what I am convinced is the "deep culture" of PE itself.

From my experience doing countless teacher workshops, teachers want a "here's how" approach. Given the circumstances they work in, that is understandable. But I refuse to treat you, the reader, as a technician. You are a professional (or soon to be one), which means that "here's how" must be accompanied by "here's what," "here's why," and "here's whether." That is to say, it is just as important to explain what teaching responsibility is about—for example, it's not about disciplining kids (although that's a by-product of becoming more responsible)—why it is important, and whether it is something you want to try (it's not for everyone). Another way of expressing this point is that, although teaching certainly has a "technology" that involves specific skills and strategies, it also ought to have a spirit—a moral compass, a sense of purpose, a passion, a vision. Ian Culpan, who spearheads PE curriculum reform in New Zealand, told me that he doesn't want a competent teacher; he wants an inspirational teacher. So do I. I want (and kids need) an imaginative, creative teacher who can go beyond connecting the dots to creating the dots (another of Culpan's ideas).

Having said that, in this edition I have tried to give you specific guidance on putting the idea of taking personal and social responsibility into practice in in-school PE. I have retained some of the alternative structures for working with kids that appeared in the first edition, but they are reconceptualized as possibilities for implementation by PE teachers.

This edition retains many of the KidQuotes and chapter-opening quotes of the first edition, and it includes a few new ones. I have edited and retained some of the sections of the first edition that continue to be relevant. But don't mistake this as a thinly disguised first edition; if you do, I will have wasted the five months I spent reworking it!

I must clarify some terminology. The approach I describe in this book is often referred to as the responsibility model or the personal-social responsibility model. In the last edition I avoided the term *model*, because some academics complained that model meant "blueprint" rather than "set of ideas." Because my intention is to present a set of ideas, I used *TPSR*, for taking personal and social responsibility, to refer to this approach. Since the last edition was published, I have reverted to using *responsibility model*, because that's what most users call it. But I've retained *TPSR* for this edition to provide some consistency for those of you who have read the first edition.

Acknowledgments

There is no such thing as an individual. We have an illusion of self-sufficiency, but actually other people support us throughout the entire process of our development.—Urie Bronfenbrenner

So many friends, colleagues, and students—those university students on my Urban Youth Leader Project staff as well as kids in some of the most underserved neighborhoods in the city—have supported me in this work over the years that I don't know where to begin. Fortunately, my acknowledgments in previous books saluted many of them. This time around, I want to particularly thank three deans (of all things) at the University of Illinois at Chicago for being supportive beyond the call of duty: Dean Vicki Chou of the College of Education, whom I mentioned in the last edition; Dean Creasie Hairston of the Jane Addams College of Social Work; and Dean Wim Wiewel of the College of Business (quit arching your eyebrows!). Also, where would I be in these past few years without Bond School principal and vice-principal Penny Kerr and Paul Butler, current and recent doctoral students Dave Walsh and Paul Wright, or my five youth-leader partners—Nick, Tom, James, Jim, and Missy? To all of you and some whom I've forgotten to mention, a way big thanks!

Part 1

IDEAS

Chapter 1

WHAT'S WORTH DOING?

Never doubt that the efforts of one person can change the world. Indeed, it's the only thing that ever has. —Margaret Mead

What's worth doing in school physical education is a question Tom Templin and I raised over a decade ago (Hellison and Templin 1991). Another way of stating this question is this: What kind of professional contribution do I want to make? The more aware I become, the more I realize that these questions have driven my work from the beginning.

WHAT'S WORTH DOING IN YOUR PROFESSIONAL LIFE?

You may find it compelling to teach kids to enjoy an active lifestyle, to teach them about the excitement of competitive sports, to help them understand how to take care of their bodies, or to teach other related topics. The list goes on. Over the years physical education teachers have been handed a bewildering array of purposes, goals, and objectives both locally and nationally. If you teach in a physical education department, you must deal with your colleagues' answers to these questions.

Science cannot answer these questions. Research can give us some idea of what works but not what's best for kids. What's worth doing probes your beliefs and values about life, kids, and physical education.

Some PE teachers and many curriculum planners both locally and nationally have a simple answer to this question: everything! They want development in fitness, motor skills, cognitive knowledge, and they want to meet an abundance of affective and social goals. At least that's the impression I get from reading many of these documents.

Less Is More

My response to this surfeit of physical education goals is to draw on Ted Sizer's (1992) less-is-more admonition: If you try to do everything, you're likely to end up with kids exposed to a bunch of ideas and content but achieving little development in any of them. That's not to say that you can't accomplish more than one goal, but however many goals you base your teaching on, kids ought to improve in each of them.

Problem Setting

One way to approach what's worth doing is as a process of problem setting and problem solving (Lawson 1984). What problems do your kids face? How can your physical education program help them? Because your beliefs and values matter a lot—or as Maxine Greene (1986) wrote, the believing and cherishing of the teacher cannot be ignored—I would add this to the problem-setting process: You need to sift and sort through these problems to determine not only which problems important for the kids can be addressed in PE but also which ones resonate with you.

I have had one significant advantage in answering the question about what's worth doing—as a university professor teaching PE to kids on a part-time basis, I've had more latitude in choosing my own path.

BIRTH OF TAKING PERSONAL AND SOCIAL RESPONSIBILITY

In its earliest form, taking personal and social responsibility (TPSR) was a survival response to the attitudes, values, and behaviors of the underserved kids I was teaching in high school physical education. It was also a clumsy effort to problem solve. I had gravitated to teaching high school students who were unmotivated and hostile because of my experience as an officer in the Marine Corps working with court-referred and other tough young men. What I wanted to do, the kind of contribution I wanted to make, involved some flimsy version of building these kids' character. So when I got out, I went back to school, became certified to teach physical education, and as a rookie university professor, volunteered to teach a class of 53 city high school boys who had flunked PE, only about half of whom showed up on any given day.

Armed only with some vague notions about building the character of these so-called at-risk kids, I set out to change the world. As resources I had what to me were exciting activities, such as boxing and weight training, as well as (or so I thought) my charming self. But I no longer had a student-teacher mentor or the authority of the Marine Corps to back me up, and my naivete was soon exposed. I wasn't charming enough, and when the kids started throwing the boxing gloves at each other, it became abundantly clear that the activities weren't working either.

Lawson's (1984) definition of problem setting included being motivated by something that threatens our ideals; that certainly explained my feelings of frustration in my first PE teaching experience with underserved teenagers. My ideals, just emerging and not yet fully formed at that time, were about building character and helping kids who were experiencing some of society's most difficult social conditions and problems. I wanted to address the social problems I could—poverty and the racism of a white society were out of reach—by somehow building character, but I was failing miserably.

I needed a much clearer purpose and set of goals as well as some intervention strategies, and quickly! I came to realize that helping my students to take more responsibility for their own development and well-being and for contributing to the well-being of others was perhaps the best contribution I could make, especially given the personal and social problems my students faced. Any external control I might impose would be transient at best, and they would still have to figure out life for themselves, if they could, without much help from social institutions. Law enforcement would do the rest, a dubious proposition at best.

If taking personal and social responsibility were to be the purpose of my program, I needed to connect it to everything we did in the gym so that while my students were doing fitness activities or learning a motor skill or whatever, they would also be learning something about taking personal and social responsibility. By doing this, I could also address motor skills and fitness development. But TPSR was too vague to help me plan a specific lesson. I still needed a better grasp of what I meant by being responsible. I also needed some specific strategies for putting this purpose into practice. What do students need to take responsibility for? And how do they go about taking this responsibility?

I couldn't see how I could avoid teaching values, a term with unfortunate emotional baggage, especially for public school teachers. As Puka (1987) pointed out, Hitler assumed enormous responsibility, but his values were immoral and antisocial. The key, I reasoned, is to treat the values not as absolutes but as qualities to

I. **Respecting the rights and feelings of others**

II. **Effort**

III. **Self-direction**

IV. **Caring and helping**

Figure 1.1   Initial version of responsibility levels.

experience and reflect on. Students are ultimately responsible for adopting, modifying, or rejecting these values in their lives.

I selected two values related to personal well-being—effort and self-direction—and two related to social well-being—respect for others' rights and feelings and caring about others. I wanted to give attention to being both personally and socially responsible. This personal-social balance can be precarious, as illustrated by the split of John Dewey's followers into two sects after his death, one child-centered and one society-centered (Jones and Tanner 1981).

Following Sizer's less-is-more principle, I had to exclude many other possible values, such as self-esteem, cooperation, and honesty (except by implication). If I wanted students to remember the values, let alone become involved in trying them out, the values had to be simply stated, concise, and few in number.

To simplify my approach further, I placed my choices in a loose progression (see figure 1.1), referring to them as awareness levels (Hellison 1978) or developmental levels (Hellison 1985). Students thus learned a vocabulary as well as a sequence, and I was able to sidestep the term *values*. As long as I was flexible in its application, this progression

- helped me plan my lessons,
- helped kids focus on issues of respect and motivation right away, and
- helped them identify self-direction and helping others as higher values.

Rationale for Teaching for Affective and Social-Moral Goals

From my many conversations with teachers over the years, it is clear that most are driven more by values and beliefs than by data-based evidence. My university colleagues, on the other hand, lean the other way. For those who want more discussion of the issues my approach to teaching raises—that is, character development, social problems, and teaching values—I briefly discuss them here.

Character Development

Past and present sport, exercise, and physical education leaders have often claimed that a number of personal and social benefits result from participation in physical activities. Sport builds character. Running makes you feel better. Play fair in class and you will play fair in life. The list goes on.

Unfortunately, these claims far outdistance the evidence (despite the personal testimonies at athletic banquets). Although research supports some of these statements, it does not support others, and the evidence often points in different directions (Fejgin 1994; Gruber 1984; Shields and Bredemeier 1995; Willis and Campbell 1992).

This is not to say that the potential for personal and social benefits is nonexistent. It's just risky to assume that such outcomes automatically accrue from participation in sport, fitness, or physical education. Changes in participants' feelings, attitudes, values, and behaviors are more likely to occur if someone, whose presence reflects the desired qualities, plans and exemplifies them.

Physical activity instructional settings hold the potential for such development because as environments they are emotional, interactive, and, for some kids, attractive. Life in the gym provides seemingly unlimited opportunities for intervention and for the demonstration of personal and social qualities, not only in games but also in exercises, drills, discussions, and informal student actions (which may include inactions). As one social worker told me, kids "show more of themselves" in physical activity settings, and in the gym or on the playing field, intervention can be more closely tied to immediate experiences than it can in traditional therapy sessions.

Nel Noddings (1992, 48) points out the potentially holistic nature of physical activity programs:

> [T]he physical self is only part of the self. We must be concerned also with the emotional, spiritual, and intellectual self, and clearly these are not discrete. We separate and label them for convenience in discussion but it may be a mistake to separate them sharply in curriculum.

Despite this potential, progress will be difficult if professionals in the field believe that personal and social benefits accrue automatically as the result of participation in physical activities, or cling to a narrow "physical self" view of what ought to go on in physical activity programs. Progress depends on clearly conceptualizing what we mean by personal and social development (or building character or even fair play) and then developing strategies and teacher qualities that promote these concepts. Those of us who talk about the potential contributions of physical activity programs to the personal and social development of young people need to do both—conceptualization and strategy development—if we want to go beyond mere claims.

Fortunately, some educators have done this kind of work. Examples include character development (Beedy and Zierk 2000), cooperation (Bressan 1987; Orlick 1978), moral development (Gibbons, Ebbeck, and Weiss 1995; Shields and Bredemeier 1995), sportsmanship (Giebink and McKenzie 1985; Horrocks 1977), and social responsibility (Horrocks 1978; Trulson 1986).

Conceptualization and implementation are difficult because personal and social development involves more than a list of specific behaviors. Personal and social behaviors, such as working independently, helping someone, or cooperating with a group, are easy to identify; but attitudes, values, beliefs, feelings, and self-perceptions matter as well. How someone feels—an intangible mix of perceptions and intentions toward the self or someone else—may have greater personal-social implications than more visible behaviors. Wright (cited in Arnold 1988, 35) puts it this way:

> [A person] cannot be defined through an inventory of actions performed [but rather] by a description of the principles that give coherence and meaning to an individual's behavior, and of the relatively enduring dispositions that underlie it.

It is as if both an inside self and an outside self are present in all of us, one very visible, the other existing mostly below the surface (Thomas 1983).

Social Problems Perspective

The "surge of social pathology" (Csikszentmihalyi and McCormack 1986, 417) among youth in recent years is reflected in escalating statistics for school dropouts, drug abuse and trafficking, delinquency, teen pregnancy, gangs, suicide, violence, and vandalism. Although there is some controversy over interpretation of the data (Caldas 1994; Hodginson 1991; Ianni 1989; Ralph 1989; Walberg, Reyes, and Weissberg 1997), it is quite clear that more children and youth are at risk.

These trends have been blamed on more families becoming dysfunctional (with increased incidence of child neglect and abuse, homelessness, and "kids raising kids"), on the increased availability of drugs and guns, on images from television and other media, and on social, political, and economic conditions, including poverty, racism, and joblessness, which have made war zones of the areas in which many low-income families live.

Certainly, the growth of a disenfranchised underclass accounts for some of the problem. Few people question that inner-city kids are growing up in environments that put them at risk. As Kunjufu (1989, 48) observed, "We have youth who are being killed because they stepped on someone's shoe or brushed up against someone in a crowded hallway between classes."

All inner-city families are not dysfunctional, however, and some kids who grow up in underserved neighborhoods become productive parents and citizens, and distinguish themselves in their chosen line of work. Moreover, kids who are at risk of being affected by social problems live not only in the inner city. A principal of one of the most affluent suburbs in the Chicago area has estimated that 50 percent of the families in his school district are dysfunctional. Aggregated data for all youth reflect a substantial rise in crime, violence, sex, and drug use (Lickona 1991). As Benson (1997, 3) observed, "These concerns cannot be dismissed as urban issues alone. Part of the American dilemma is that these issues affect all sizes of communities."

Institutions that have traditionally provided support and guidance for children and youth do not seem to be able to respond adequately to these trends. The Carnegie Corporation Task Force on Youth Development and Community Programs (1992) concluded that community programs designed to serve adolescents are not reaching most of the kids who are unsupervised after school and most likely to harm themselves and others. McLaughlin and Heath (1993) also found that most inner-city community programs and policies do not respond to the needs of kids; the programs are, for the most part, not developmental, not empowerment oriented, and not focused on the whole person.

In public schools, teachers face the escalation of crime, violence, sex, and drug use as well as depression, attempted suicide, and school absenteeism (Benson 1997). According to Des Dixon (1994),

KidQuotes

"This class helps you become a better person."—Eighth grader

"He teaches you the main points about life."—Eighth grader

schools compound the problem by treating kids as if they live in a *"Leave It to Beaver* world," as passive, dependent, incapable.

American kids are receiving less support and guidance in a society that bombards them with more choices than ever before and places many of them at a social, economic, and political disadvantage from the start. It is no wonder that many feel alienated and powerless and turn to withdrawal or rebellion.

Teaching of Values

Teaching values, even in the context of individual responsibility, raises the specter of indoctrination. I was uncomfortable with this possibility from the outset, but I needed several years to develop and implement strategies that effectively shifted responsibility to students.

Although I struggled in my experiences and in my mind to find ways of teaching that could convey values without resorting to indoctrination, others have provided support. Tappan (1992, 387) argued that proponents of universal conceptions of morality need to address the problem of employing "techniques of indoctrination to transmit certain values [rather than encouraging] students to discuss, examine, and reflect critically on values and ethical positions within a diverse, complex, and ever changing society." Mary Bredemeier's (1988, 223) study of urban teachers also refuted the indoctrination approach. Her work showed that successful teachers have a strong commitment to help their students make "choices and . . . deal with the consequences," develop a "sense of control over one's own behavior," and accept "responsibility for one's acts." Sizer (1992, 59) also was critical of school practices that "infantilize and pamper their students . . . [an approach that] thwarts opportunities for young people to take responsibility, to develop the habit of delivering on that responsibility . . . [and denies] opportunities to practice those habits." Kamii, Clark, and Dominick (1994, 673), following Piaget, saw the development of autonomy as the one broad aim of education, defined as "the ability of an individual to be self-governing in the moral as well as intellectual realm."

deCharms (1976) conceptualized these viewpoints theoretically by arguing that we must help people to become origins in their lives. By this he meant teaching them how to set internal standards, including doing as one must rather than as one pleases and striving for goals in the face of opposing external forces, although this striving may not always pay off. deCharms believed that being an origin has a moral dimension, because it requires us to take responsibility for the consequences of our goals and to treat others as origins rather than as pawns to be manipulated. deCharms demonstrated the power of these ideas by implementing them in inner-city elementary schools and collecting data to demonstrate their effectiveness.

A society based on democratic principles, however uneven their application, depends on people who can make thoughtful decisions, people who have had practice in decision making. As Jones and Tanner (1981, 497) noted, "training children for freedom requires other kinds of plans and structures than training them for slavery." Moreover, as Romig (1993, 316) pointed out, "the essence of morality is the ability to choose well." In a society of increasing choice and decreasing guidance, this ability to choose well, to make thoughtful decisions, becomes even more important.

Cultivating the decision-making process involves giving young people the opportunity to share their beliefs and knowledge and to test these ideas in a controlled forum. Such experimentation is good not only because it follows a democratic perspective but also because it reveals that students know things that teachers don't know. In an increasingly diverse society, in which teachers are often of a different subculture than their students, giving students the power to apply their special knowledge of their world to make decisions can lead to better decisions and a better education. As an added benefit, the process of sharing decision-making power also raises the important question of who has the power to determine what is of value in a diverse society.

Giving students responsibility yields psychological benefits. As Alfie Kohn (1993, 11) put it: "All else being equal, emotional adjustment is better over time for people who experience a sense of self-determination." Instructors benefit as well because there is less occasion for the "I tell you what to do and you try to get out of doing it" game that teachers and students often play.

For all these reasons, helping students take personal and social responsibility in part means sharing power with students and shifting decision making to them. TPSR does not mean getting inside kids' heads but getting them inside their own heads.

THERE ARE NO SILVER BULLETS IN PHYSICAL EDUCATION

TPSR is no panacea for the social problems we face today. Pete Mesa (1992), superintendent of schools in Oakland, California, outlined three levels of causes engendering social problems:

- Root causes, such as poverty, racism, inadequate health care, inadequate parent education, and lack of opportunity

- Intermediate causes, including the need for skills in and a disposition toward social competence, problem solving, autonomy, and a sense of purpose and future
- Immediate causes, such as guns in schools

In Mesa's conceptualization, I focus on intermediate causes. My approach, to the extent that it works, is one small piece of the puzzle. Weiner (1993, 2) persuasively argued that none of this intermediate work will make much of a difference "unless social and economic relations are utterly transformed, and that process will take a sustained, vigorous struggle by all who recognize the inequality and injustice of the status quo."

Although by root causes Mesa meant broad societal economic, educational, and social problems, Dill (1998, 40) viewed the school culture as a fundamental problem, despite years of reform efforts: "The role of the public school is to produce graduates who are decent people. But schools are not currently organized to accomplish that task." For this reason, full implementation of TPSR and other affective or social-moral approaches is often difficult in schools.

Even as an intermediate approach, TPSR is just one of many. Alone, it is not going to save the world. Other PE curriculum approaches that hold promise include cooperative games (Orlick 1978), Built-in Dilemma-Dialogs (Romance, Weiss, and Bokoven 1986), adventure education (Hattie, Marsh, Neill, and Richards 1997), sport education (Siedentop 1994), Fair Play for Kids (Gibbons, Ebbeck, and Weiss 1995), and Sport for Peace (Ennis, Solmon, Satina, Loftus, Mensch, and McCauley 1999). Even those hard-core martial-arts instructors who not only expel their students from the program but also cut up their earned belts in front of the class if they violate their no-drugs policy may be making an important contribution outside school walls.

TPSR stands for a set of ideas that have grown out of my attempt to help at-risk kids take more responsibility for their personal and social development in physical activity settings. Although no panacea for today's social problems, providing today's young people with guidelines for, and practice in, taking responsibility for their personal well-being and contributing to the well-being of others can make a difference in what they value and what choices they make.

Take-Aways

Here are some things from this chapter that you might consider taking with you:

- As a physical education teacher, what's worth doing is perhaps the most important question you can ask yourself. The question takes on added significance if we cannot provide our students with developmental experiences in all the goals advocated locally and nationally. The answer: You can't do everything; therefore, less is more.

- I developed TPSR as my answer to what's worth doing. TPSR involved making good on my commitment to helping kids with the social problems they face and to help their personal and social development, thereby unavoidably requiring that I teach values.
- There are no silver bullets in teaching physical education! That includes TPSR. Because your answers to what's worth doing may be different from mine, you may not find TPSR right for you.

Chapter 2

THEMES FOR TEACHING PERSONAL AND SOCIAL RESPONSIBILITY

No more prizes for predicting rain. Prizes only for building arks. —Louis V. Gerstner Jr.

When I visit gyms of teachers who tell me they are teaching their students to take personal and social responsibility (TPSR), I am often greeted by a wall chart announcing the "Levels of Responsibility" followed by four numbered descriptions of specific behaviors. My knee-jerk reaction is to wince, not because of what the teacher is doing with students—I don't know what he or she is doing—but because of the images such posters immediately conjure up in my mind.

What bothers me is that although the four "levels of responsibility" do represent four of the five responsibilities that I ask my students to take on (and the fifth one was absent in my early work), the more I work with TPSR, the deeper I seem to get into its essence, perhaps akin to peeling an onion (or preferably an avocado). I continue to learn more about what becoming personally and socially (and morally) responsible entails, which then informs and gradually transforms my teaching practices. I'm sure that's why I tend to recoil at the interpretation of TPSR as four levels of behavior. To me it's so much more than that. To be fair, many teachers understand that but work under severe constraints that limit the implementation of a full-blown version of TPSR. Moreover, evidence (Mrugala 2002) suggests that many teachers start with the four levels of behavior but, according to their own testimonies, become more holistic teachers as they use the four levels, even though that wasn't their intention.

Wall charts are fine and often helpful to students (see chapter 3), but what I hope to convey to you in this chapter is more of the spirit or essence of TPSR. The following overview of the goals and themes of TPSR can provide you with a vision, a distant goal, toward which you can then begin to move in a series of sequential stages. The wall chart shown in figure 1.1 (on page 6) is expanded and briefly explained (see table 2.1). I then describe four themes that, if they are a consistent presence in all TPSR lessons, will facilitate application of the goals or levels.

FIVE GOALS

The five goals shown in table 2.1 help both you and your students focus on what students need to take responsibility for. Although taking responsibility for your own development and well-being and for contributing to the well-being of others is the purpose of TPSR, the five goals give students specific responsibilities, specific targets to shoot for, within the broader purpose. Chapter 3 explains each of these goals more fully. The point here is to introduce you to a more authentic version than that shown in figure 1.1 on page 6.

These goals are often referred to as levels because they represent a loose teaching and learning progression from one to five. Although students don't always progress in a linear fashion, the levels provide specific steps in planning lessons and in making personal plans for individual students.

The first two goals (or levels), respect and effort, can be viewed as the beginning stage of responsibility development; both are essential to establishing a positive learning environment. The next two, self-direction and helping, extend the learning environment by encouraging independent work, helping roles, and leadership roles, thereby freeing you to work with kids who need more help and, at the same time, contributing to a more positive experience for all students.

Transfer outside the gym is the most advanced stage; it involves exploring the previous four responsibilities in school, at home, with friends, and so on to evaluate whether they work better than what the student has been doing. Unfortunately, teachers often exclude this goal.

Teachers often stress the behavioral nature of the levels. That makes sense because they deal with behaviors all the time, and some of them interfere with teaching and learning. But TPSR encompasses more than observable behaviors; it also includes attitudes, beliefs, values, and intentions. In other words, it takes into account the inside self as well as the outside self. Focusing exclusively on behaviors, while easier, restricts us to the tip of the iceberg. Fortunately, strategies are available to make the inside self more accessible (see, for example, group meetings and reflection time in chapter 4).

Table 2.1   The Components of the Levels

Level	Components
I	**Respecting the rights and feelings of others** Self-control The right to peaceful conflict resolution The right to be included
II	**Participation and effort** Self-motivation Exploration of effort and new tasks Courage to persist when the going gets tough
III	**Self-direction** On-task independence Goal-setting progression Courage to resist peer pressure
IV	**Helping others and leadership** Caring and compassion Sensitivity and responsiveness Inner strength
V	**Outside the gym** Trying these ideas in other areas of life Being a role model

From "Teaching for affective learning in physical education," L. Masser, 1990. This article is reprinted with permission from the Journal of Physical Education Recreation and Dance, 1990. JOPERD is a publication of the American Alliance for Health, Physical Education, Recreation and Dance, 1900 Association Drive, Reston, VA 22091.

A number of goal modifications are available to suit a variety of teaching situations and teacher perspectives, including the popular "cumulative levels." I will describe these in the next chapter as part of an in-depth treatment of TPSR goals.

SOME BUILDING BLOCKS IN USING PHYSICAL EDUCATION TO TEACH RESPONSIBILITY

Although the levels of responsibility occupy center stage for most TPSR teachers, four themes are essential to guide the understanding and implementation of this approach; the next section describes them. First though, I will describe some building blocks that provide the foundation for TPSR in physical education.

- Physical activity programs offer unique personal and social development opportunities, and claims are often made about the contributions they make. But personal and social development is not automatic; progress requires specific goals, strategies, and teacher qualities (see chapter 1).
- If physical education is to be truly developmental and holistic, it needs to be focused as well. Following Sizer's (1992) less-is-more guideline, a program with a few goals will have more effect on kids than one with many goals.
- Because physical activity is central to physical education, you must be competent in teaching physical activities. That is, you must have both content knowledge and pedagogical skills. It's not enough to be good at teaching responsibility, just as in TPSR it's not enough to teach physical activity well.

FOUR THEMES

The purpose of a theme is to provide consistency across lessons, units, physical activities, and the like—in other words, to be a constant presence in your program after the first few weeks of getting started (see chapter 9). The following four themes, because they represent the essence of teaching personal and social responsibility, should be present in the lessons of any teacher who professes to practice authentic TPSR.

Integration

The TPSR levels and strategies must be integrated into the physical activity lesson rather than taught separately. You must therefore be competent not only in teaching physical activities but also in teaching students to become more personally and socially responsible—and in integrating the two sets of content. In truth you need to master three sets of content—physical activity knowledge, physical activity-related pedagogical skills, and TPSR—and be able to integrate the three in a seamless way.

A different approach, which I call the add-on, is common. Here the teacher may teach a lesson on basketball in which kids, following the lead of highly visible professional athletes, do their share of intimidation and cheating during the game despite the teacher's valiant efforts to minimize such behaviors. After the game, the teacher lectures on sportsmanship or has kids role-play conflict resolution. Role playing conflict resolution in PE is unnecessary because the game provides plenty of conflicts to do the real thing. The same holds true of sportsmanship as well as many other attitudes, motives, and values that emerge during the class. Teachers tend to teach skills as an add-on as well by having students practice the correct form, and they then allow regression to a less effective but more familiar form during the game. In both cases, the teacher does not plan for integration.

Transfer

After using TPSR in my teaching for almost 20 years and mindful of the less-is-more guideline, I hesitated to add a fifth level. But when I realized that transfer is really the ultimate point of teaching kids to take personal and social responsibility, I had to build transfer into the goals or else leave it to chance. All along, my sense of purpose, my vision, my passion has been to help kids lead better lives. Their lives don't end when they leave the gym. Kids can learn to take responsibility in PE, but transfer from the activity setting to other arenas of life such as school, playground, street, and home is not automatic. We must teach it just as surely as we need to teach respect for others in PE.

There are lots of ways to teach for transfer. For example, when you talk with a classroom teacher of one or more of your students, ask how your student(s) is (are) doing with self-control or effort. Then tell your kids that you sometimes ask their teachers how responsible they are, and perhaps tell them what the teacher said, good or bad, but without the teacher's name. You can also ask them by a show of hands how responsible they are in class or on the playground.

Empowerment

Lickona (no date, 2) captured the essence of empowerment:

> Choices determine our quality of life. You get to choose: how to treat other people, how much you'll learn, how you'll handle adversity, your character—the kind of person you'll become. It's an inside job.

I would only add that our genetics, circumstances, and socialization enhance or restrict our ability to choose. With effort and guidance we can overcome some of these hurdles, as the resiliency literature demonstrates, but freedom of choice is not unrestrained.

TPSR stands for taking personal and social responsibility as Lickona suggests. That's why I often use terms like *self-control, self-motivation,* and *self-direction* in the levels and sublevels. The implication is that these are the students' responsibility. You therefore

KidQuotes

"In here we're treated like people."—Fourth grader

"This class makes the world a better place."—Third grader

"On a 1-to-10 scale this class is infinity."—Eighth grader

become a facilitator, gradually shifting power from yourself to students until they are doing more and you are doing less. In actuality, your role just shifts from direct instruction to guidance. Facilitating and providing guidance means helping students learn to make wise personal and social-moral decisions and giving them opportunities to do so, accompanied by self-reflection.

Of course, nothing is simple when it comes to dealing with the complexity of human beings, as Joe McDonald (1992) so eloquently pointed out in his book *Teaching: Making Sense of an Uncertain Craft.* Empowerment is an uneven process. Your class, as well as individuals within your class, may take on considerable responsibility one day and regress the next. Students may show little interest for several weeks (or months) and suddenly show signs of controlling their temper, learning independently, or even stepping up to leadership roles.

A number of strategies are available to help students to make their way through the empowerment process. Chapters 4, 5, and 6 describe these approaches. For example, group meetings and reflection time (see chapter 4), which are built into the daily lesson plan, help students evaluate the lesson and their role in it, with the purpose of making them more aware of what they are doing and whether it is in line with their own goals as well as the goals of the class.

Another strategy is the accordion principle. The teacher can give both the class in general and individual students more or less responsibility to carry out any of the levels. My rule of thumb is to empower the whole class gradually and build this idea into my lesson plans. At the same time I know that some students can move along the empowerment continuum faster than others, for example, by working on their own at a station or by providing some peer leadership for a drill. I also know that some won't be ready to assume the extent of responsibility I'm asking of the class; they need a more structured situation. Reducing empowerment sometimes becomes an issue, for example, when I replace a student leader who has slacked off. Sometimes they don't want to hear the reasons, but that too is part of their responsibility. Letting out and squeezing in the accordion with all the accompanying problems comes with the territory of empowerment (see chapter 6 for strategies to deal with these problems).

Schilling, Martinek, and Tan (2001) use this developmental continuum for youth empowerment:

1. Students share their ideas and thoughts in the group meeting.
2. Students make decisions within the physical activity program.
3. Students engage in peer teaching and coaching.
4. Students take on leadership roles with younger kids, that is, cross-age teaching.

Teacher-Student Relationship

None of these things matter if you don't develop a certain kind of relationship with your students. Although much has been written about this issue (for example, McDonald 1992; Noddings 1992; Tom 1984), it is still too often perceived as either a mixture of artistry and charisma or, in contrast, a set of concrete pedagogical skills. Although I expand on this relationship in chapter 7, the key is being able to recognize and respect the following qualities in one's students (imagine them entering the door to the gym):

- Each has strengths, not just deficiencies that need to be fixed. (Who wants to be fixed?) Sure, we all need work to be better human beings. But by recognizing and building on strengths, students are more likely to be open to working on their issues, such as making fun of others, getting angry when things don't go their way, being a good team member, and so on.

- Each is an individual and wants to be recognized as such, despite the uniformity of attire, slang, gestures, and so on. Gender matters, of course, and so does race and ethnicity. (Whoever said, "It doesn't matter to me if they are green or blue," just didn't get it.) But I've never met a kid that wanted to be known as a category. She may be proud of being a girl or a Mexican American, but that's not all she is. And kids are not just a bundle of behaviors. They have an inside self that contains feelings, dreams and fears, values, intentions. Of course, most kids don't want to stand out in ways that they or their peers judge to be "uncool" (although those seeking attention are another matter), but they do want to be recognized and respected for who they are. That's where recognizing kids' strengths and potentials comes in.

- Each knows things the teacher does not; each has a voice, an opinion, a side, that needs to be heard. When I first got the idea to listen to what kids think, I only had in mind to convey to them that I cared about their thoughts. What I found was that they know things I don't know and often evaluate things differently than I do. Listening to them made me a better teacher!

- Each has the capacity, if not the experience, to make good decisions. Often, they just need practice, as they do in learning a motor skill. If given the opportunity, they will make mistakes, but that's an important part of the process. Self-reflection needs to accompany decision making; it is built into the daily lesson plan (chapter 4) to help students become more reflective about the choices they make.

But in implementing TPSR, why is it necessary to recognize and respect these particular qualities? TPSR is about treating kids with dignity and promoting holistic self-development and human decency. If you want to treat kids with dignity and promote self-development, working from kids' strengths shifts the focus from their inadequacies and incompleteness to their positive qualities, which provide a base from which to work. Recognizing and respecting their individuality conveys to them that everyone starts in a different place and has unique strengths, capacities, needs, and interests. As Walt Manning used to say, "You gotta treat them unequal but fair." This admonition runs counter to the notion that teachers need to treat everyone alike, and it's more difficult to pull off. Regardless, honoring differences among students is what individuality is all about. Giving students a voice in the process and turning some choices and decisions over to them are central to promoting empowerment. And what better way is there to treat kids with dignity, to model human decency?

This won't work if you only go through the motions. Instead, you must "teach individuals, not classes" (Dill 1998, 66) and truly believe that each student comes to you as an individual with strengths, with a voice that needs to be heard, and with the potential for making wise decisions. As I've already admitted, I didn't start listening to kids because I believed they had something to say; that realization came after I began to listen. It may be, as some argue, that behavior precedes belief, that if one behaves as if they care about this or that, they will begin to do so. I'm doubtful about that, given the wide variation in human thought and action, but you may need to start that way. If so, keep track of your true beliefs to see if they change. If not, TPSR may not be right for you.

ROLE OF THEMES

If these themes need to run throughout your programs front to back and top to bottom, they should run throughout this book as well. Count on it.

- Transfer is described as Level V in chapter 3, and strategies for transfer are suggested in the lesson-plan format in chapter 4 and in the integration of Level V in the physical activity lesson in chapter 5.
- Integration of personal and social responsibility with the physical activity lesson is described in detail in chapter 5.
- Empowerment runs through every chapter, even in the sections on solving discipline problems in chapter 6 and evaluating and grading students in chapter 8.
- The teacher-student relationship is described in detail in chapter 7, facilitated by a counseling-time strategy in chapter 4.

But first, what so many teachers consider to be the essence of TPSR, the levels of responsibility, are described in detail in chapter 3.

Take-Aways

Here are some things that you might consider taking with you from this chapter:

- The levels of responsibility are built on a foundation of building blocks and themes. To ignore these is to risk missing the point of TPSR.
- Unless your daily interactions with your students embody and demonstrate the principles of TPSR, nothing else matters.
- If you don't gradually empower your students, taking personal and social responsibility (TPSR) becomes a slogan without meaning.
- Unless you integrate TPSR into your physical activity lesson, the majority of your lesson and central reason for physical education is likely to teach kids not to take responsibility.
- If you ignore Level V, transfer to life outside the gym, you will not fulfill the original purpose of TPSR, to help kids with their social problems and build character.

Chapter 3

LEVELS
OF RESPONSIBILITY

No philosophy, theory, or theorist can possibly capture the idiosyncratic reality of your own experiences as a teacher.
—S.D. Brookfield

Language is always a problem in communicating ideas to others. Because so many teachers use the term *levels of responsibility,* I will do the same. But understand that these levels are program goals derived from the more generic purpose of teaching kids to take responsibility for their own development and well-being and for contributing to the well-being of others. For years now, I have simply used the term *responsibilities* as when I say to my students, "These are your responsibilities."

The five levels shown in table 2.1, page 17, define for students what responsibility means and what they are to take responsibility for. The levels were formulated to meet the following needs in teaching young people to take personal and social responsibility:

- To be simply stated and few in number
- To balance personal and social responsibility
- To indicate a progression (though not a strict one)
- To be provisional in nature

The term *provisional* in this context means that the validity of the values offered in TPSR depends ultimately on acceptance, rejection, or modification of the values by the student. This is called empowerment.

Progression of Levels

In my experience, having some sense of what to do first, second, and so on is helpful not only in program planning but in teaching values to kids. In planning, respect for the rights and feelings of others is necessary before much else can be addressed. Participation and effort in the program, especially in its physical activity content, is usually the primary reason for having the program, so it needs to be addressed early on. Self-direction, which involves working independently and eventually making and carrying out personal plans, comes next in the sequence because it is more difficult. For most kids, genuinely caring about and helping others is yet more difficult because it involves going beyond one's self-interest and becoming less egocentric. Most difficult of all is transferring these values and skills outside the gym, where the environment is often less supportive.

Respect for the rights and feelings of others is perhaps the least each of us can do for others, just as putting effort into the tasks we take on is perhaps the least we can do for ourselves. Becoming self-directed is an advanced stage of personal responsibility, and appropriately caring about and helping others is arguably the most we can do for others (and perhaps ourselves as well).

A less rigid way to present the levels progression, which I personally favor, is as a sequence of three categories: beginning, advanced, and most advanced (see table 3.1).

The order of the levels attempts to take into account both a loose teaching-learning progression and a hierarchy of values. When Williamson and Georgiadis (1992) worked with kids from the notorious Cabrini Green Housing Project, they needed to spend the first few weeks exclusively on Level I to deal with issues of violence and abuse. Respect was a minimal value that required immediate attention and therefore needed to be the first step in their instructional plan.

The progression, even when defined as loose, is open to question. For example, Shields and Bredemeier (1995) suggested moving caring to Level II and reconceptualizing Level III as group direction.

Table 3.1   Levels Progression As a Sequence of Three Categories

Category	Levels
Beginning	Level I, Respect Level II, Participation
Advanced	Level III, Self-direction Level IV, Caring
Most advanced	Level V, Outside the gym

Their aim was to de-emphasize what they perceived to be the egocentrism of the levels. The Saskatchewan, Canada, provincial curriculum guide inverted the levels so that what the committee thought was the most important level, caring about and helping others, came first. The appropriate caveat is to use the progression flexibly. If it becomes a rigid, dogmatic structure within which kids must fit, whether they really do or not, or if it is used as a weapon to beat up kids when they don't conform, then the intention that created the levels has been lost.

Although a balance between personal and social-moral responsibility is reflected in the progression, the primary focus is on the individual taking responsibility rather than the group, as Shields and Bredemeier pointed out. However, some Level IV and group-meeting strategies do address group responsibility (see chapters 4 and 5).

CUMULATIVE LEVELS

When I was in survival mode as a teacher in the early 1970s, I began to teach the levels as a cumulative progression, as shown in figure 3.1. Used this way, students learn that each level builds on and encompasses all lower levels. A new level, Level Zero, represents irresponsible attitudes and behaviors. Level I becomes respect for others' rights and feelings without participation in the lesson's activities (and without self-direction or caring about others). Students at Level I show minimal social responsibility but no personal responsibility. Level II describes a participant who participates under supervision and respects other kids' rights and feelings. Level III represents someone who is respectful, participates, and is self-directed. Level IV adds helping and leadership to the traits of Levels II and III, and Level V signifies that a student is trying out and practicing Levels II, III, and IV outside the gym.

The cumulative approach has the advantage of simplicity, which is why I created it. Students can quickly set goals for themselves, such as to achieve Level III or Level IV (thanks to Karyn Hartinger for this example), and they can quickly evaluate themselves—for example, by saying, "I was mostly at Level II today." The disadvantage is that students are often at several levels in one lesson. They may call someone a name but then help someone later; they may be off task at one moment and self-directed the next. Some teachers have created rules for self-evaluation. For example, students who were at more than one level that class period must evaluate themselves at the lowest of these levels. Using that rule, any student displaying Level Zero behavior is on Level Zero for the lesson. Students in one of my

Level IV, Caring

Students at Level IV, in addition to respecting others, participating, and being self-directed, are motivated to extend their sense of responsibility beyond themselves by cooperating, giving support, showing concern, and helping.

Level III, Self-direction

Students at Level III not only show respect and participation but also are able to work without direct supervision. They can identify their own needs and begin to plan and carry out their physical education programs.

Level II, Participation

Students at Level II not only show at least minimal respect for others but also willingly play, accept challenges, practice motor skills, and train for fitness under the teacher's supervision.

Level I, Respect

Students at Level I may not participate in daily activities or show much mastery or improvement, but they are able to control their behavior enough that they don't interfere with the other students' right to learn or the teacher's right to teach. They do this without much prompting by the teacher and without constant supervision.

Level Zero, Irresponsibility

Students who operate at Level Zero make excuses, blame others for their behavior, and deny personal responsibility for what they do or fail to do.

Figure 3.1　The levels presented as a cumulative progression.

Adapted, by permission, from D. Hellison, 1985, Goals and strategies for teaching physical education (Champaign, IL: Human Kinetics), 6–7.

programs invented a scoring system of their own to deal with this problem. They averaged the different levels they were on for a given lesson and came up with a cumulative level (for example, two and a half) to represent their various attitudes and behaviors.

The cumulative approach has other disadvantages as well. Most cumulative-level users completely ignore Level V. Its inclusion does raise issues—students need to provide evidence from outside the gym—but ignoring it minimizes the life lessons of TPSR. The other disadvantage involves the temptation to use the cumulative levels to label students. It's almost too easy—one number will do the trick. But the point of empowerment is for kids to evaluate themselves. Our role is to raise questions when necessary and share our evaluations when appropriate but not to force our judgments on students. They are the only ones who can change themselves (Boyes-Watson 2001).

Five Levels

Although I abandoned the use of cumulative levels within a few years, it remains a popular choice for many teachers. As I dug deeper into each of the levels and began to appreciate their nuances, it seemed best to treat each separately. The components of each level are shown in table 2.1, page 17. To minimize the chance of getting lost in these details, it may help to remember that the essence of Levels I and IV is human decency, just as the essence of Levels II and III is self-development.

Level I

Level I, respect for the rights and feelings of others, is intended to provide a psychologically and physically safe place for students and to confront students who need to deal with issues of self-control and respect. The major problems that Level I attempts to address are

- verbal and physical abuse, such as name calling and making fun of others;
- intimidation, bullying, and hogging equipment or space;
- inability to control one's temper or to resolve conflicts peacefully; and
- disrupting the work and play of others.

Students who struggle at Level I often deny personal responsibility and make excuses or blame others for their own abusive behaviors. Students sometimes acknowledge being abusive or manipulative but argue that the behavior is justified in a survival-of-the-fittest world. Interestingly, both affluent kids and street kids use this kind of explanation on occasion.

Level I has three related components. The first, self-control, means controlling one's attitude and behavior in a way that respects the rights and feelings of others. I tell kids it means controlling your temper and your mouth, two of their major problems. Moreover, the person does so without supervision (or policing). Self-control is an external behavior that may not be matched by the internal value of respecting others, a crucial but often overlooked distinction. To learn respect for others, students can start by trying to control self-ish behaviors while they struggle to become internally more sensitive to others' feelings and needs.

Self-control means not being controlled by what others say. It does not mean giving away one's rights. In some cases, when someone's behavior does not deserve respect, self-defense may be the only alternative. But as Walter Mosley's fictional detective Easy Rawlins said in *White Butterfly*, "I want you to promise me that you won't never fight unless somebody hits you or tries to hit you. 'Cause you know that some man can control you if he can drive you to fight over some [garbage] he talks." Responding in kind to abusive words or behavior must occur only in situations when it is absolutely necessary. I've seen students attempt to retaliate to the talk of others only to be further humiliated. And retaliation encourages more retaliation. Where does it end? All too often these days it culminates in injury or death.

The second component of Level I, the right to peaceful conflict resolution, encourages negotiation and recognizes that legitimate differences of opinion can sometimes make rights difficult to determine. This component helps students learn the value of resolving conflicts peacefully and democratically (see chapter 6).

The third component specifies that everyone has the right to be included. All participants deserve turns and playing time, whether or not they are skilled and regardless of gender, race, ethnicity, or sexual preference.

As with the other levels, Level I is not an either-or, yes-no proposition. A continuum exists between having no respect for others to full, internalized respect. Students are present all along this continuum, and their attitudes may fluctuate from day to day. Socialization into elitist values or street values is a barrier to the development of Level I. In my experience, however, all students (or almost all) can make progress on this continuum and improve their day-to-day consistency. If progress is not possible, the right to exit the program (or referral to a specialist in cases of genetic or behavioral disorders) should be available. A developmental perspective makes these last-resort courses of action less likely.

Level I can be viewed as the least any of us can do for others, whereas Level IV, caring, can be seen as the most that we can do for others. Empathy, taking the perspective of another, begins at Level I and develops further at Level IV.

Level II

Just as Level I attempts to counter socially destructive attitudes, values, and behaviors, Level II, participation and effort, is intended to help students positively experience program content. Participation counters self-defeating attitudes and behaviors, such as the passivity of "cruisin' in neutral," learned helplessness (Martinek and Griffith 1993), and attempts to discredit anything that appears to have meaning (Maddi, Kobasa, and Hoover 1979). Level II is also intended to help students better understand the role of effort in improving oneself not only in physical activity but in life.

The first component of Level II is self-motivation because the intention of Level II is to help students take responsibility for their own motivation. Shifting some small responsibilities to students in skill drills and fitness activities, such as moving to the next station when they have finished a task, can greatly facilitate the development of self-motivation.

Exploring effort and trying out new tasks acknowledge the importance of experimentation and tiptoeing into unfamiliar territory. This could be called "Try it, you might like it!" Simply going through the motions of participation is a first step past nonparticipation. Gradually, the concepts of training and practice can be introduced, leading to feedback in the form of development in such things as motor skills and game play as well as physical health, physical appearance, and strength. For development to occur, however, the third component of effort, the courage to persist when the going gets tough, often needs to be invoked. Tom Martinek explains Level II by saying, "Try your best and don't give up" (thanks to Tom for this example).

Exploration at Level II also needs to include introduction to a variety of personal definitions of success. By exposing your students to a variety of definitions of success, they can eventually develop internal standards that work for them. Competitive achievement is initially the most popular definition of success, but improvement, achievement of personal goals, or even effort can define success. John Nicholls' (1989) theory of task versus ego involvement sheds light on this component of Level II. A task-involved person defines success in terms of participation, improvement, and mastery in a specific task, whereas an ego-involved person defines success as being superior to others. With task involvement, success depends primarily on one's own effort (although there are other factors such as ability and task difficulty), whereas in ego involvement, success depends on how others do. Kids need to understand their options and be able to put them into practice.

Level III

Level III, self-direction, is intended to help students go beyond the lessons of Level II as they learn to take more responsibility for their well-being. Level III celebrates the diversity of student talents, needs, and interests by encouraging reflective choice. Level III promotes a "complementarity of excellences" (Norton 1976), treating all responsible self-direction goals as equal rather than favoring culturally popular activities, one gender over another, or the motor elite.

You may wonder whether Level III is relevant for children. My experience with primary and elementary school teachers is that, although some of the ideas described here are too advanced, children can often do more than we expect. Such things as goal setting may be relevant if adjusted for age, for example, by introducing the idea or giving some choices with reflection afterward.

The first step at Level III is to move from the more teacher-directed confines of Level II to on-task independence, such as by working at a station without supervision. The next step is to begin a goal-setting progression that will depend on your kids' ages, self-motivation, and understanding of the goal-setting process. Goal-setting principles are a staple of sport psychology (Weinberg and Gould 1999) and include setting goals that are realistic and under the student's control. Students should also record their progress. You can set goals for students until they grasp the idea. Eventually, they should be able to make and carry out a personal physical activity plan. To set, carry out, and evaluate personal goals requires self-knowledge (such as "What do I need to improve on?") and conceptual knowledge (such as the role of feedback in motor skill improvement).

Level III also involves working toward an understanding of one's needs, not just one's interests. Setting goals and self-standards and developing one's uniqueness (for example, by developing a physical activity specialty) are aspects of this process. Of course, having fun, being with friends, celebrating, and even managing stress are important too. Even though most kids are oriented to the present, learning to choose and stay with activities that meet both long- and short-term interests and needs in some balance is one of the hallmarks of mature self-direction.

To accomplish the kind of independence required for true self-direction, students must develop the courage to look inside them-

KidQuotes

"The levels were good. They let you know if you were acting like a fool or whatever."—High school student

"I know I have responsibility as a person and you helped me find it."—Seventh grader

selves. Some of this is sensitive work, especially for adolescents. If you can convince students to bring perceived weaknesses out into the open, they can address the need to look good or seek approval by making personal plans to strengthen those weak points. Many students would feel better about themselves if they confronted their issues and made a plan to resolve them, either by self-acceptance—accepting limitations that make them less popular while emphasizing being oneself and developing one's talents—or by self-image actualizing (Lyon 1971), which involves making and carrying out a plan to improve skills, game play, strength, endurance, appearance, or whatever is necessary to feel better about oneself.

Among the most difficult aspects of striving against external forces is being able to stand up for personal rights. Creating a truly personal plan, derived from one's own needs and interests, is no easy task for kids who need peer approval. You can address the importance of making a plan that is truly one's own in awareness talks, group meetings, or counseling time (described in the next chapter). Having identified their needs as something distinct from the opinions of others, students also need to learn how to stand up for their independence and protect themselves. A plan to do so may take the form of learning how to be appropriately assertive and practicing such assertiveness in the physical activity setting (Banks and Smith-Fee 1989) or even learning self-defense skills. Outward Bound creator Kurt Hahn put it this way: We need to "make the brave gentle and the gentle brave" (Richards 1982). Making the brave a bit gentler is the aim at Level I, but Level III helps the gentle become brave.

Level IV

Level IV, like Level III (and all levels), needs to be adjusted for age. Mature Level IV students possess the interpersonal skills of sensitivity and responsiveness, act out of caring and compassion for others (a process started at Level I), contribute to their community, and do so without expectations of extrinsic rewards. Working at Level IV is easier said than done. It requires the interpersonal-relations skills of listening and responding without being judgmental or dogmatic, helping without being arrogant, helping only if the other person wants the help, not becoming a rescuer, and learning to help others resolve differences peacefully and democratically. Students at Level IV need to recognize that others have needs and feelings just as they do, and they must learn to see and feel things from the viewpoints of others.

Despite the emphasis on sensitivity and compassion in Level IV, interpreting it as being soft would be a mistake. Level IV requires inner strength—the courage to resist peer pressure and one's egocentric agenda, to step up as a leader. Leadership requires not only the skills and qualities mentioned earlier but also the ability to balance the task of giving a group direction with facilitating their needs and interests. It requires confidence but not arrogance as well as the ability to strive against external forces (deCharms 1976) when necessary.

Interpersonal skills aside, Level IV may be a difficult achievement for young people these days. Thanks to the electronic media, celebrities have the kids' attention more than ever before. One teacher who includes a hero unit in her curriculum has said that it is becoming harder to teach the unit because kids can't distinguish between a hero and a celebrity (Lickona 1991). From a Level IV perspective, a hero is someone who shows extraordinary courage and compassion in contributing to society. Perhaps Kirby Puckett, who said that winning the Branch Rickey Award for Community Service meant more to him than anything he has done in baseball, clarifies the difference between celebrity and hero.

Whether Level IV really extends beyond self-interest in its broadest sense is a matter of debate. Not at issue, however, is the importance of being a contributing member of the community and society. William James argued that kids need to find "a moral equivalent to war" as their sense of purpose (Richards 1982). Kurt Hahn (Richards 1982) and others (notably Berman 1990) have suggested offering students opportunities to make social contributions as this moral equivalent.

Level I and Level IV attempt to counter ego- and ethnocentrism, the me-first and us-first orientation that inspires all the "isms"—racism, sexism, motor elitism, handicappism, ageism (Siedentop 1980). Level I teaches doing no harm; Level IV teaches making a positive contribution. The emphasis of Level IV on contributing to the well-being of others balances the self-centered goals often chosen in Level III.

Level V

Level V refers to application of the four other levels outside the program—on the playground, at school, at home, on the street. A wall chart developed by Michigan elementary PE teacher Linda Masser (1990) addressed the transfer issue by showing students how the levels apply to different settings in their lives (see figure 3.2).

If students are to become responsible for their well-being and that of others, they need to be the ones to decide whether and in what situations to use the levels. Level V makes students aware of the possibility of transfer and encourages them to discuss it. For example, Gene Washington, a university basketball player who

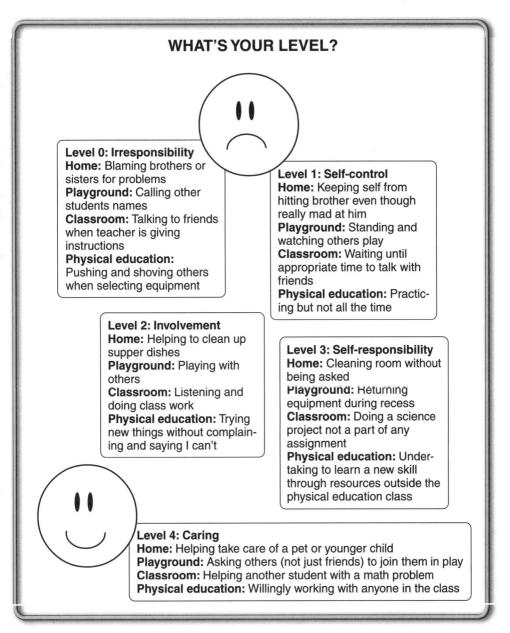

WHAT'S YOUR LEVEL?

Level 0: Irresponsibility
Home: Blaming brothers or sisters for problems
Playground: Calling other students names
Classroom: Talking to friends when teacher is giving instructions
Physical education: Pushing and shoving others when selecting equipment

Level 1: Self-control
Home: Keeping self from hitting brother even though really mad at him
Playground: Standing and watching others play
Classroom: Waiting until appropriate time to talk with friends
Physical education: Practicing but not all the time

Level 2: Involvement
Home: Helping to clean up supper dishes
Playground: Playing with others
Classroom: Listening and doing class work
Physical education: Trying new things without complaining and saying I can't

Level 3: Self-responsibility
Home: Cleaning room without being asked
Playground: Returning equipment during recess
Classroom: Doing a science project not a part of any assignment
Physical education: Undertaking to learn a new skill through resources outside the physical education class

Level 4: Caring
Home: Helping take care of a pet or younger child
Playground: Asking others (not just friends) to join them in play
Classroom: Helping another student with a math problem
Physical education: Willingly working with anyone in the class

Figure 3.2   Linda Masser's application of the four Levels in various settings.

From "Teaching for Affective Learning in Physical Education," by L. Masser, 1990, Journal of Physical Education, Recreation and Dance, *61, p. 19. Reprinted with permission of the* Journal of Physical Education, Recreation and Dance. JOPERD *is a publication of the American Alliance for Health, Physical Education, Recreation and Dance, 1900 Association Drive, Reston, VA 22091.*

assisted me in an inner-city program, told the kids that self-direction helps improve both their individual basketball skills and their schoolwork.

Level V is the place to discuss the reality of life outside the gym. Within the program, the levels contribute to a climate of respect, effort, autonomy, and community, but these qualities are not often valued on the street or even at home and at school (especially in the halls, lunchroom, and on the playground). It is one thing to work on them in a safe setting where everyone is respected and has a say, but what if someone out there is not respectful or is downright out of control? What if that person is an adult? What if others ridicule your effort because someone else can shoot the ball better or because putting effort into schoolwork is not cool? What if a kid doesn't go along with the crowd? Level V can't solve these problems. It can't, for example, make weaker kids stand up for their rights on the playground. But you can discuss these issues during awareness talks, group meetings, and counseling time, giving kids a chance to think about the relevance of the levels for their lives outside the gym. What would it take to put them into practice? Is it worth the effort? The students can also volunteer examples, perhaps about how they took responsibility on the playground.

Level V ultimately means being a role model for others. Charles Barkley caused quite a stir when he said that professional athletes are not role models. I tell kids that rather than look for role models, be one. TPSR is one way to give them the tools to do that.

LEVEL MODIFICATIONS

The five levels—respect, participation, self-direction, caring, and transfer outside the program—can be represented in different ways. Missy Parker's fourth-grade Navajo students called Level II "work and try" and Level III "just do it" (with apologies to Nike; thanks to Missy for these examples). In a team sport unit, these cumulative level substitutions were used (Hellison and Georgiadis 1992):

- 0 = Cut from the team
- I = On the bench (no problems but not participating)
- II = Player (under supervision)
- III = Self-coach
- IV = Coach
- V = Outside the gym

Levels can be deleted, rearranged, split apart, or supplemented. Darin Kennedy, a primary school PE teacher in Falconer, New York, uses color-coded levels including yellow for following the Golden Rule and red for having "heart" (thanks to Darin for this example). Curt Hinson (1997; 2001) used three levels in adapting TPSR for recess and playground (see chapter 10):

1. Unacceptable
2. Acceptable
3. Outstanding

The Saskatchewan provincial curriculum inverted the levels so that caring and helping was number one. In basketball I changed Level II, effort, to teamwork, because the kids wanted to play basketball but weren't interested in passing the ball or cooperating.

Other approaches similar to the TPSR levels may work better for you. John Hichwa's wonderful book on middle school physical education, *Right Fielders Are People Too* (1998), described his three Rs for teaching prosocial behavior:

1. Respect (for example, consideration of others)
2. Responsibility (for example, obligation and accountability)
3. Resourcefulness (for example, having the inner strength to accomplish something)

Hichwa posts the three Rs and discusses them every day. In addition, they are an integral part of his daily lesson plan. For example, two small groups of students play games by themselves, taking responsibility for working independently, calling their own fouls, and including everyone. Meanwhile he works with a third small group, "giving individualized instruction and adding variation to the activity" (p. 41). Such small-group interaction allows him to personalize his teaching and motivate his students.

The guiding principle for using the levels or some other approach effectively is to make sure they make sense in your setting and serve your purpose.

RELATION OF LEVELS TO THEMES

The levels provide specific targets for student empowerment. Levels II and III are aimed at having students gradually take responsibility for their own well-being, whereas Levels I and IV focus on their contributing to the well-being of others. Level V addresses transfer.

The levels will remain words on the wall chart unless you develop a teacher-student relationship conducive to teaching responsibility. If your students feel that you see their strengths, treat them as individuals, and empower them to share their views and make decisions, a number of things begin to happen. You introduce them to Level I by treating them with respect, and you set up Level IV by treating them with caring, sensitivity, and responsiveness. By your recognizing their potential for empowerment, students begin to accept the idea of taking responsibility. And by honoring their strengths and individuality, you lay the foundation for Levels II and III.

The integration of the levels with physical activity awaits the strategies in chapter 5.

Take-Aways

Here are some things from this chapter that you might consider taking with you:

- The levels provide students with specific targets for taking responsibility.
- The levels are intended as a loose progression, both for planning your lesson and for progressive steps the kids can take.
- Cumulative levels can be helpful to beleaguered teachers because they simplify a complex process. They often omit transfer, however, an especially serious flaw in full implementation of TPSR (as discussed in chapter 2).
- Empowerment must be linked to the levels so that students evaluate themselves and begin to take responsibility for their own well-being and for contributing to the well-being of others.
- Difficult as this is, you should not reduce the levels to behaviors. They also represent the students' inside selves—their values, intentions, motives, and attitudes.
- The levels are "social constructions," which simply means that you can modify them in all kinds of ways as long as you remain true to the underlying principles of TPSR, including less is more.

Part II

STRATEGIES

Chapter 4

LESSON PLAN

Education worth the name is essentially education of character. —Martin Buber

Day-to-day consistency in the use of the four themes and levels of responsibility is an essential feature of TPSR. Despite the plethora of curriculum objectives and school policy edicts, effective learning requires that we cover less but go in depth more, which is why less is more is a core concept in Sizer's (1992) Coalition of Essential Schools. I've found that it takes a lot longer for something like respecting the rights and feelings of others to sink in with students than I initially thought. And even then their understanding is superficial, and their values and behaviors are slow to catch up.

One way to achieve some consistency in using TPSR is to use a daily format for your lessons—that is, to fit your specific lesson for the day into a routine that students experience in class after class. The daily format I have used for years consists of five parts:

1. Counseling time either before or after the lesson (or at other times)
2. An awareness talk to open the lesson
3. The physical activity lesson itself with TPSR woven into the instruction
4. A brief group meeting near the end of class so that students can express their opinions about how the class went and how to make improvements
5. Reflection time to close the class so that students can evaluate how personally and socially responsible they were that day

COUNSELING TIME

Because the teacher-student relationship is crucial to making TPSR work, connecting one on one with kids is essential. The challenge is doing so with little time and large classes. Still, somehow you need to convey to each student that he or she

- has strengths as well as things that need work,
- is a unique individual,
- has a voice that matters, and
- has the capacity to make decisions.

The daily format itself helps to reinforce these student qualities— for example, when students conduct awareness talks themselves (see "Awareness Talk," page 43), express opinions in group meeting, and evaluate themselves in reflection time—but nothing substitutes for a quality one-on-one exchange with you, even if it is brief.

Before or after class, a quick sentence or exchange can begin to communicate these things. Raths and his associates (1966) called this a one-legged conference, meaning a quick exchange as you're walking by. If you schedule a bit of Level III time before class and have equipment out, your conversations can be extended a bit more (while you walk around taking roll if necessary). Conducting counseling time after class permits you to follow up individual student successes and problems immediately that day.

If you are an elementary school teacher and have little time available before or after class, you will need to try to find those moments during class, on the playground, or at lunch when you can make a brief one-on-one connection. You can also do counseling time during a scheduled Level III time for all students, when they work independently at stations, play games, or carry out their personal goals and plans. Even if you only make, say, five of these contacts a day, not counting kids chronically in trouble, they mount up and make a difference. You should try to keep track of whom you've already talked with so that, in the long run, you leave no one out.

In such a brief encounter what can you accomplish? Here are some possibilities:

- To recognize and show respect for student strengths, mention a talent you notice (especially if it is not generally acknowledged) or comment on a recent effort, improvement, or achievement. You could comment on fitness and skills, of course, but you could also connect the levels to areas outside physical education, such as academic progress. You might note that the student helps make the gym a more positive place, helps other students, and provides leadership. You can remind students who struggle with one or more of the levels of the need to work on these problems and the potential they have to improve.

• To recognize and show respect for individuality, just check in and comment on a facial expression (smile or grimace) or a new hairstyle or an item of clothing. Commenting on their individual strengths, efforts, improvements, and achievements as suggested earlier also recognizes individuality.

• To recognize and show respect for students' voice, ask authentic questions (not questions that require a certain answer) and show genuine interest in their answers, comments, and questions. Ask them if they have a solution to a problem that has come up in the group meeting or in the lesson, whether or not they are involved in the problem—such as how to help some kids manage their anger, how to stop arguments in games, how to improve the class's motivation, how to get leaders to step up.

• To recognize and show respect for students' capacity to make decisions, notice choices they have made and comment on them or ask whether that choice worked for them. Ask their opinion about solving class problems as suggested earlier, and ask kids who seem ready if they would like to take on a Level III or IV task that day or in the near future.

Counseling time, as a term, raises a question about whether you and I are really therapists in disguise. People have argued the point from both sides. A TV interviewer once accused me of being a PE shrink trying to get inside kids' heads. I replied, being oh-so-cool under pressure (ha ha), that I was just trying to get kids inside their own heads. I like Noddings' (1992) claim that all decent adults should be prepared to educate kids morally, that it is a human responsibility. Tom agreed when he described teaching as a moral craft (1984). I also like this dictum from Quincy Howe (1991, 3): Social workers can "address part of the job, but a teacher can address the entire job." Of course, this responsibility holds true only to a point; professional help must sometimes be sought. If a student's problem runs deep or seems to require specialized skills, a referral is the appropriate choice.

AWARENESS TALK

Next, you bring students together, standing or sitting, and briefly teach the five responsibilities. You should do this gradually in most settings, beginning with respect and effort, eventually adding self-direction and helping, and even later including transfer outside the gym. The awareness talk must be brief. A couple of quality minutes of talk is worth far more than blabbering on and on. Teachers who are long-winded, a characteristic common among rookies, often obscure their message in a torrent of words. Early in my career, I got a wakeup call from one of my students who wrote "You talk too much" on an anonymous evaluation form. Monitor your students' eyes and adjust accordingly.

Following the initial teaching, the awareness talk is an opportunity to remind students about their responsibilities that day. After students learn the levels and have some experience with them, you can call on them to conduct the awareness talk, describing what the program is about in their own words (rather than mimicking the teacher). They need not say everything, but whatever they say should indicate that they grasp in at least a general way what TPSR is about. Kids come up with some doozies. One third grader said this, without his teacher having ever uttered these words: "This class is about making the world a better place to be!" An inner-city seventh grader surprised his teacher even more by saying, "It's having a philosophy!" (thanks to Dave Walsh for these examples).

Increasing awareness was the first strategy I used to put the levels into practice. I quickly learned that awareness wasn't enough, but I also learned that it helped, especially when I curtailed my long-windedness. These simple guidelines came out of my experience:

- Post the levels on the gym wall for easy reference. (This is the all-too-familiar wall chart, but it does help.)
- Relate the levels to current experiences in the program.
- Develop one-liners (or two-liners) to explain the essence of the levels. Here are some examples of awareness talk one-liners:
  - "The only person you really get to change is yourself" (Boyes-Watson 2001, 18) (relevant for all levels, especially Level I).
  - "You can't get to a good place in a bad way" (Boyes-Watson 2001, 18) (Level I).
  - "If one person is out of balance, so too is the community" (Boyes-Watson 2001, 19) (Levels I and IV).
  - "If people can get to you with their talk, they can control you" (Level I).
  - "To get better you have to pay the price" (Level II).
  - "You're about to spend 40 (or whatever) minutes of your life in here; what are you going to do with that time?"

- "It's your body and your life" (Levels II and III).
- "You can choose what your friends are doing or make up your own mind" (all levels).
- "Good idea, but can you say it more positively?" (Level IV).
- "Let's see if we can help everybody walk out of here today feeling that they had a positive experience" (Level IV).
- To kids whose lives revolve around basketball and dreams of the NBA: "When the air goes out of the ball, what are you going to do?" (thanks to Jimmy Jones) (Level V).
- "How could you use the levels in your classrooms? At home? On the playground?" (Level V).

Bill White, a Portland, Oregon, high school teacher, encouraged Level V awareness in his program by means of a piece of paper taped to the wall. On the paper he had drawn a line with a 0 at one end and a 70 at the other, representing ages in the life span. He drew an X on the line to represent the approximate age of his students (about 14), and on the bottom Bill had printed: "It's your trip." Bill referred to this drawing often in his awareness talks to remind his students that they had not gone far in their life "trip" and that the levels might serve as handy guides from this point onward (thanks to Bill for this example).

One way to deepen students' awareness is to ask them to help to devise respect rules for the class. How do they want to be treated? How should everyone be treated? Does name calling matter? Should everyone on a team have to be involved during a game? Should mean faces be allowed during a conflict? You could even chip in how you'd like to be treated. Students can brainstorm these issues and perhaps come up with some respect rules they can all agree on. The point is to have students think about the respect issue and give their input. To reduce the hassle of separate respect rules for different classes, Lickona (1991) suggested one set of respect rules for all programs developed from students' input in each of the classes.

Nick Compagnone (1995) extended the awareness talk into the lesson by using finger signals. When one or more students started to show disrespect, he held up one finger as a reminder to get under control. Extending this approach, one could use two fingers to signal being off task, three fingers to use independent time wisely, and four fingers to be more positive when helping someone.

The Lesson

The majority of time is spent on the physical activity lesson. During the lesson you use instructional strategies to integrate teaching responsibility with teaching the physical activities. This often means changing long-standing patterns of teaching physical activities. Be aware that integrating the levels into the lesson will probably make your teaching more difficult at first, but if you persist, your teaching will become easier. When kids start to work independently and provide leadership for other students, you can step back and give support except in dealing with kids who haven't understood or bought into TPSR yet.

Teachers can integrate awareness talk reminders into the lesson. Bill White was a master at this. He once asked a student to demonstrate the bench press, and when the student had difficulty executing a repetition, several boys laughed. One, however, quietly went over and moved the pin so the demonstrator could complete a repetition. Without missing a beat, Bill asked his students what cumulative level the laughers were at. "Zero," they mumbled. And at what level was the boy who moved the pin? "Four," several said in unison (thanks to Bill for this example).

Although empowerment is a fundamental theme of TPSR, direct instruction can be useful, particularly while students are still learning to take on some responsibilities in class. For example, respect for the rights of others involves, among other things, including everyone in the activities. Because the kids with better skills generally get the ball more in team sports, thereby strengthening their skills while ignoring the less skilled, a temporary rule might be that everyone (or a certain number) has to touch the ball before the team takes a shot on goal or plays the ball over the net. They learn not only to include others but also to use some team strategy as well, such as getting open to receive a pass or bump-set-hit.

You can integrate individual empowerment into the lessons in many ways, some simple and some more complex. In all cases you need to empower your students gradually while applying the accordion principle as needed to enlarge or reduce the extent of choice in relation to students' interest and ability to handle it. For example, you can ask students to do as many push-ups as they can instead of performing a set number, a task that does not typically recognize individual needs.

You can integrate group empowerment by taking time to teach students how to solve conflicts. You will easily recoup lost activity time once students begin to put these lessons into practice. For example, teach your kids to call time-outs during games for a brief team huddle to deal with problems.

These and many more awareness, direct instruction, individual empowerment, and group empowerment strategies that teachers have used are described in some detail in chapter 5.

GROUP MEETING

As Clark Power (2002, 134) observed, "We have little experience deliberating in common about the rules and policies that affect our daily lives, and often less experience deliberating about the common good." The group meeting gives students practice in these democratic values and skills.

Near the end of the period, students gather around you, standing or sitting depending on the time available. The purpose of the group meeting is to give students the opportunity to express their views about the day's lesson, how their peers as a whole did, and perhaps even how effective your instruction and leadership were. They can also raise issues and suggest possible solutions, or you can suggest a solution and ask for advice. You can discuss problems that students have with one another during counseling time or, if you handle it carefully, during group meetings. I emphasize repeatedly that blaming others is not appropriate for group meetings or in class, that instead students need to express how they felt and how what others did affected them. Then we can discuss the issue, and I can talk individually with the students who are implicated. Sometimes humor works. In response to a complaint from a boy about two girls trying to play basketball with him, Nikos Georgiadis responded: "I don't see two girls; I see two basketball players" (thanks to Nikos for this example).

If time is limited, you cannot effectively use many of these group-meeting strategies. One possibility is to ask for one or two volunteers to say what they liked or disliked about the class that day, perhaps followed by a show of hands of those who agree. In that way at least students will have a chance to share their points of view.

An important purpose of group meetings is to give students practice in the group decision-making process and to experience the feeling that they can make a difference through a group process. Decision-making abilities improve gradually, and, as students gain practice, they become more competent at making group decisions, evaluating the program, and coming up with ideas for improvement. When I first asked my students how I could improve, they didn't understand the question! All group-meeting strategies could be new to students, depending on how other teachers in school and other adults in their lives treat them. But they probably have the least experience in formally evaluating adults in their lives, especially if the person they are evaluating is requesting the evaluation. As your students learn that you want their input and that you won't be judgmental about what they contribute, the trust between you and your students will improve, and they will feel more comfortable in sharing their true feelings and opinions.

Group-meeting strategies primarily focus on Levels I and IV, Level I because the problems addressed usually involve respect issues, such as disruption, conflict, and abuse, and Level IV because the whole process can be viewed as a contribution or service to the group, the program, and the teacher. As one self-centered student complained, "Why do I have to do this? It's not my problem." The process demands a caring perspective, caring about the program and about others in the program. But it is also self-serving, and this point is not lost on students. If they want things their way, they need to lobby for their interests. This process, often contentious, can lead to students' seeing someone else's side of an issue and becoming more empathic, even if only slightly. Levels II and III aren't altogether excluded from group-meeting strategies because the content of Level II (drills, workouts, scrimmages, games) and the quality of Level III time can be topics for discussion.

After experiencing TPSR for a while, students ought to have the opportunity to comment on the levels—to suggest modifications, additions, and subtractions in relation to the levels you have been using in class. You can introduce this question early and hold brief discussions from time to time. You should emphasize their reasoning in this process and encourage them to be more reflective about, and empowered to do something about, systemic change. Again, this transfers to life, where systemic change is needed to address deeply rooted social problems (see chapter 1).

Of course, tradition and experience often intrude when students analyze the levels, which is why this assessment should come after they have had some experience in TPSR. One time a group of students decided they wanted to play trash-talk, in-your-face basketball. This decision violated Level I, but we talked about it and voted. Trash talk won by a couple of votes. I agreed that during the next lesson they could split into groups and play basketball "their way," but by the end of the lesson the groups had called time-out on their own and decided to reinstate Level I. Such a happy conclusion was by no means assured. If they had not made that decision, I would have been back to the drawing board. When you give students the opportunity to make decisions that matter, the decisions they make may not support TPSR. This possibility is part of the process. The levels are, after all, provisional values, not mandates. The progression to full decision making needs to be gradual, but at some point you should address conflicts between program goals and student goals.

Although Level V, outside the gym, is mostly the province of reflection time, sometimes things do come up in group meeting—an upcoming exam that has a strong bearing on whether students will move on to the next grade (in these test-oriented times), a new dress code, a squabble in the lunchroom, in-school suspensions. These things are often big deals to kids, and you need to acknowledge them.

In some programs, teachers use workbooks or journals to give students the opportunity to evaluate the class as well as themselves. Writing in private sometimes elicits opinions that students are reluctant to express with their peers. In our martial-arts programs, students comment on the class, evaluate their responsibilities, and keep track of their fitness and skill progress in a workbook.

Occasionally, when something happens that requires immediate attention of the whole class, you can hold group meetings on the spot. In most cases, however, holding a group meeting just before reflection time at the end of class provides a better time for sharing perceptions of the class that day.

Rules for all meetings—the end-of-class group meeting, team meetings, conflict resolution meetings, and so on—are based on Level I:

- No disrespect in the discussion, for example, no ganging up (Meadows 1992) or blaming others
- Inclusion of everyone in the discussion
- Peaceful resolution of conflicts

REFLECTION TIME

The last activity students engage in before they leave gives them an opportunity to evaluate their attitudes, intentions, and behaviors in relation to the levels. Whereas the group meeting empowers students to evaluate the program, reflection time is designed so that students can reflect on and evaluate themselves—that is, how well they respected others' rights and feelings, the extent of their self-motivation in class activities, their self-direction if you give them the opportunity, their contribution to others and to making the class a positive experience for everyone, and whether they put some of these things into practice outside the program.

A variety of self-evaluation methods are available. The simplest one, if you treat the levels separately (instead of cumulatively), is to use thumbs pointed up, down, or sideways for each level. For example, the question "Who didn't make a problem for anybody else since you came into the gym?" asks kids to point their thumbs upward (I didn't cause anyone a problem), sideways (I caused some minor problems), or down (I need work on this). Before you go to Level II, look around to be sure everyone is pointing their thumbs and to get an idea of how the class in general saw themselves that day in relation to that level. Using hands to indicate yes or no is an even simpler evaluation system, although it is less accurate because the only choices are good or "not yet." Brief journal entries permit students to keep their self-evaluations and explanations private (see form 4.1). To validate the process, however, you have to read their comments and write something back (or at least initial their entry), and this takes time. Some teachers do one class a day, thereby reducing the written work to read every day yet offering their students the opportunity to express themselves privately once in a while. Checklists provide a written shortcut to journals. Workbooks, which include other self-evaluations such as fitness and skill development, are an effective way of doing reflection time. Karyn Hartinger in elementary school PE and Jeff Walsh in middle school have used this approach, and so have I. Nick Cutforth and Missy Parker (1996) wrote a useful article on journal writing in physical education, arguing that it doesn't need to take much time and can be beneficial to both teachers and students.

Level V, in which students transfer values outside the gym, calls for a slightly different question: "Did you do any of the levels outside of class since we met last? If so, how did it work?" I've found that the application of the levels outside the gym is often too general for kids to grasp. A better approach is to ask students to volunteer examples of how they have used one or more of the levels in their lives outside PE. One of my students recently answered, "Yeah, I'm not getting suspended so much!" Another way is to ask a specific question, such as one of the following:

- "How was your self-control in the classroom so far today?"
- "How was your self-motivation in doing your homework last night?"
- "How self-directed were you after school yesterday?"
- "Did you help anybody to learn something after school yesterday or in school today?"

Students may have difficulty understanding how to transfer the levels to other areas of their lives. After all, the climate in many settings does not approach that of a TPSR gym. As one student exclaimed, "Do this stuff on the street? You've got to be kidding!" So we talked

Form 4.1

Self-Evaluation

Date _____

Self-control: How well did you control your temper and mouth today?

Effort: How hard did you try today?

Self-coaching: Did you have a self-improvement or basketball goal and work on it today?

Coaching: Did you help others, do some positive coaching, or help make this a good experience for everyone today?

Outside the gym:

Self-control?

Effort?

Goal-setting?

Helping others?

One comment about yourself today:

From Teaching Responsibility Through Physical Education,
Second Edition *by Don Hellison, 2003, Champaign, IL: Human Kinetics.*

KidQuotes

"He gave us a chance to prove ourselves, but I didn't like his big talks before class."—High school freshman

"The talks were good so everything doesn't get chaotic."—High school sophomore

"This isn't the Burger King. You can't always have things your way."—Sixth grader in group meeting

in specifics about whether students can do anything related to the levels anywhere outside the program and to what extent.

For self-reflection to work, students need to be (reasonably) honest in their responses. If they had a bad day, they need to be able to admit it without being penalized, but they also need to understand that self-reflection includes self-analysis of their excuses, especially when they blame others for things that they did or did not do. Students need to examine the reasons for, and consequences of, their attitudes and behaviors. One way to focus their attention on the consequences of their attitudes and actions is to ask, "Did what you did today work for you and why or why not?" As with the group meeting, such honesty and introspection doesn't usually happen unless they perceive you to be supportive and trustworthy.

The cumulative levels (shown in figure 3.1, p. 28) provide a simple and convenient self-evaluation system for reflection time. Students choose the cumulative level that most closely represents their attitudes and behaviors for that class period. For example, if the student views herself as having been respectful of others as well as a participant in the activities during the lesson, she would give herself a Level II. If she participated but was verbally abusive to another player, she would not have met the criteria for Level I and so would rate herself at Level Zero. They can call out the number while sitting in a circle at the end of the lesson or on their way out of the gym (thanks for this idea to Portland, Oregon, middle school teacher Jeff Walsh). Or they can hold up fingers to show their level (thanks to Reedville, Oregon, elementary teacher Tim Kramer). Another method is to ask students to make a journal entry in which they write a cumulative level for the day along with an explanation.

Pete Hockett, PE teacher at an elementary school outside Madison, Wisconsin, painted the levels vertically on his gym wall next to the door. His students simply touched whichever level they had as their goal for that day as they came into the gym and whichever level they achieved during class when they left the gym. Pete only talked with those who, upon entering the gym, touched Levels Zero or I, because that told him that they were having a bad day. He also spoke with those whose self-evaluation at the end of the day didn't quite match his observation ("I didn't notice you helping anyone; what did you do?") (thanks to Pete for this example). Kit Cody, a PE teacher outside Portland, Oregon, modified Hockett's strategy by displaying the levels in a target. When the target fell off the wall one day, his kids were so used to the routine of "touching in and touching out" that they continued touching the blank wall space where the target used to be (thanks to Kit for this example)! Tim Kramer created a tag board with pockets for his Reedville, Oregon, elementary school students. He assigns a color to each cumulative level. At the end of class kids put a colored card in their pockets to represent their cumulative level for that day. By looking at the tag board, Kramer could quickly check any discrepancy between what levels students choose and what he observed. He would then discuss this difference of opinion with the students (thanks to Tim for this example).

Ordinarily, reflection time occurs at the completion of a lesson so that students can evaluate their lesson involvement in relation to the levels. Sometimes, however, reflection time is useful during the lesson when you want students to reflect on a particular choice you have given them or a particular event that has just occurred. For example, it's easy for kids to make choices but far more difficult to make good choices. Questions such as "Did that choice work for you?" and "Would you choose that again?" can help your students think more deeply about making wise choices.

Take-Aways

Here are some things from this chapter that you might consider taking with you:

- The five-part sequential lesson-plan format provides day-to-day consistency in your students' exposure to, and experiences in, taking responsibility.
- Counseling time gives you a chance for a few one-to-one interactions.
- The awareness talk sets the stage, and the lesson puts responsibility into practice in physical activity.
- The lesson closes with a group meeting, which provides opportunities for students to share their ideas and thoughts, and a reflection time devoted to student self-evaluations of their responsibilities that day.

Chapter 5

INTEGRATING RESPONSIBILITY WITH PHYSICAL ACTIVITY CONTENT

It is impossible to distinguish between the methodology and the message. —John Goodlad

One of the four TPSR themes, the integration of personal and social responsibility with physical activity content, is the focus of this chapter. The empowerment theme, essential to teaching students how to take personal and social responsibility, is also woven throughout.

The physical activity lesson is by far the most extensive aspect of the lesson-plan format. It is also the easiest to ignore. Teachers learning to do TPSR seem more able to interject the awareness talk, group meeting, and reflection time into their lesson plans while teaching their physical activity lesson pretty much as they always have. This chapter expands the brief introduction to the physical activity lesson in the last chapter by describing specific strategies at each level for integrating personal and social responsibility into the physical activity lesson plan. First, however, let's focus on the physical activity subject matter.

PHYSICAL ACTIVITY CONTENT

Physical activity content is obviously integral to any physical activity program. But I don't want to make the mistake attributed to both John Dewey and Charles Silberman, who claimed that their approaches not only attended to the whole child but were superior ways to learn content. As Nel Noddings (1992) points out, their approaches may not teach content as well as other approaches, but students in programs of the Dewey-Silberman type are more likely to become better as people.

As I've said, TPSR levels and themes need to be integrated into the physical activity lesson. I probably manage to make this connection about 70 percent of the time (that's my view, not the kids'). The rest of the time we do activity for activity's sake, have fun, and so on. How often in a lesson you try to make this connection depends on many factors but especially your curricular goals. The important thing if you want TPSR to have a presence in your program is that kids experience taking responsibility during physical activity.

To capitalize fully on the physical activity setting as a place to teach personal and social responsibility, the physical activity instruction must be competent. Physical activity is the central and most visible feature of the program. In my voluntary basketball and martial-arts programs, kids don't come to write in journals or hold group meetings; they come to shoot three-pointers or learn a spinning back kick.

But I have had more than a few students who couldn't care less about physical activity content, and they were at both ends of the skill spectrum. I remember Cliff, who was repeating his high school PE requirement and could hardly walk across the gym floor without tripping. But once he began to grasp what the program was about—that he was respected and had a say in what went on, that the gym was a safe place to be—he was the first student to show up and the last to leave. He volunteered to put up the volleyball net and, by the end of the year, to do about a hundred other chores. Then there was David, a highly skilled kid who brought a number of problems to the gym. He wrote this in a letter to me years later:

> What I really admired about going to your classes was that if you didn't learn anything physical, you could always learn something mental. Myself, I learned more mental stuff, but that's because I could learn physical stuff whenever I wanted.

Nevertheless, had the instruction not been credible, David probably would not have made this statement. For the Cliffs of the world, and perhaps for some Davids, content is less important than how they are treated and what they learn about life. Yet many others do come for the content, and if they believe it to be poorly taught or poorly understood by the teacher, TPSR is also weakened.

Other stakeholders—perhaps including parents, administrators, students, and taxpayers—expect the instruction to be competent. A swimming teacher knows that people expect his students to learn how to swim, and a baseball coach is supposed to know how to coach baseball. So the physical education teacher should be credible to the stakeholders as well, which means delivering competent, knowledgeable instruction even if the primary purpose of the program is personal and social responsibility.

Awareness talks, reflection time, and group meetings take time, even if done expeditiously. Individual and group decision, by empowering students to negotiate and make choices, also reduces skill and fitness instruction time. These tradeoffs are necessary in teaching personal and social responsibility.

Do some physical activities facilitate TPSR more than others? The answer to this question is a qualified yes. Different forms of physical activity offer different opportunities. For example, games and scrimmages offer many opportunities for teaching social responsibilities such as leadership, teamwork, fair play, and physical and verbal conflict resolution. Fitness activities provide opportunities to develop personal responsibility for oneself, individually and noncompetitively. Less feedback is required in fitness than in skill learning, so independent work is more accessible. Volleyball is more cooperative than most other team sports because the bump-set-hit is an integral part of the game. Basketball and football, in which trash talk and an in-your-face attitude are common, and martial arts, which is sometimes associated with violence, provide opportunities to confront and discuss these values.

People have challenged me on several occasions about my use of basketball in inner-city programs because, according to detractors, basketball is an extension of street life (anger, violence, egocentric activity, sexism) and perpetuates the social-mobility myth of an NBA career. They have suggested cooperative games, adventure education, and other alternative forms of physical activity as substitutes. My response is that these alternative activities may be preferable in some situations, but if an attractive activity can be offered within a framework of personal and social responsibility, the effect on students may be greater and attendance may be better. I willingly acknowledge that as activities like trash talk become more ingrained in popular sport, it becomes more difficult to use sport as a vehicle for teaching responsibility.

As teachers, most of us are not equally competent at all activities, nor do we always have the luxury of choosing to teach only our favorite activities. I run basketball programs in Chicago, for example, because the kids want them and will show up, even if I do weird things like make them write in journals. Obviously, I present myself differently in these programs than does my colleague Nikos Georgiadis, a former professional basketball player. I have learned a lot from Georgiadis, but I can't be him. One time a student complained that he wasn't getting to shoot enough because he was required to pass to his teammates. Georgiadis asked whether the best shooter should take all the shots. "Sure," the student replied. So Georgiadis joined the game on his team and proceeded to knock down about 10 shots in a row. The kid didn't get to touch the ball in all this time. "How do you like this idea now?" Georgiadis asked during the group meeting. The student decided that getting everyone involved might be a better option.

The teacher must therefore find a personal style of teaching the activity. Demonstration by the teacher is not essential (there are other ways to get the points across), nor must the teacher play with the students. The point is that as teachers we are responsible both for knowing as much as possible about the content and for finding our own style.

STRATEGY PROGRESSION

Where do you start in integrating TPSR into your physical activity content? Chapter 9 addresses this question for the entire lesson in detail, but this brief description of getting started in the physical activity lesson will help the rest of this chapter make sense. TPSR relies on four general strategies:

- Awareness so that students become aware of their responsibilities and begin to understand what your class is really about
- Direct instruction in which you make all or most of the decisions to help your students begin to experience TPSR
- Individual decision making, which consists of an empowerment progression so that students gradually take more control of, and responsibility for, their decisions, attitudes, and actions
- Group decision making, including both the whole class and smaller groups, to deal with issues involving the group's well-being

At first, most of your lesson plan will involve awareness instruction and reminders plus direct instruction. That doesn't mean that you talk most of the time! It simply means that you hold a brief awareness talk and then intersperse one- or two-sentence reminders during the physical activity lesson. You also start using direct instruction so that students can begin to experience facets of TPSR. You might require everyone to touch the ball in a game to begin to teach the right of everyone to be included, or you might use reciprocal coaching (adapted from Mosston and Ashworth 1994) to introduce everyone to a simple way to help others with their skill development. Both of these strategies, described in more detail later, are based on decisions you make about what your students are to do and how they are to do it. Students are not empowered at this stage, but you have introduced them to respecting the rights of others and helping others as part of what physical education is about.

In addition, you can begin to introduce individual and group decision making. For example, you could use negotiation in dealing with Level I problems and give small groups, teams, or squads responsibility for making some decisions. As the year progresses, or as several years progress if you have your students for more than one year, more of your lesson can involve individual and group decision making with less awareness and direct instruction. As always, you can use the accordion principle with both individuals and the group to expand or contract empowerment opportunities as necessary.

Level I Strategies

Students who disrupt the lesson by disrespecting their peers—for example, by name calling, intimidation, or losing their temper—are addressed in the next chapter, which focuses on problems and situations that arise in class.

A different Level I issue, respecting the right to participate, can be treated not when a problem arises but by changing rules of the games being played. For example, one rule that we can change to reduce student feelings of exclusion ("nobody wants me") is the much maligned but nonetheless common practice of choosing sides. With so much criticism and so many alternatives available, it is amazing that choosing sides has survived. I'll give student coaches the responsibility of creating teams with the mandate to "make the sides fair." Because they are in a meeting by themselves, they may choose sides or use some other procedure, but at the end, they need to ensure that the sides are fair. If time is short, I'll arbitrarily group students with comments such as "It doesn't matter" and "If your team isn't as strong, take that as a challenge."

Inclusion games help students get the idea that everyone has the right to participate. For example, the all-touch rule in basketball means that no one can shoot until everyone on the team has handled the ball. The rule can be modified so that only a certain number of players on offense have to receive the ball or puck, depending on the sport or game. One sixth-grade inner-city boy who was required to play with and pass to girls responded in this way to an end-of-year questionnaire that asked if he improved as a person: "I improved because any other time I wouldn't want girls on my team!"

To modify volleyball for inclusion, the rules can require two hits on a side, and the server can move up if necessary to get the ball over the net. If students have difficulty returning overhand serves, the rules can require underhand serves. In this and other instances, you can change the rules or relax them as students' skills improve.

Softball can be modified so that all fielders (or a certain number of fielders) must touch the ball after the batter hits it. If they can accomplish this before the batter circles the bases and scores, the batter is out (thereby promoting batter fitness as well). You can further modify the game so that every batter has the opportunity to put the ball in play, for example, by giving students who have difficulty hitting a pitch the option of using a tee. You can do the pitching yourself to control ball speed for different batters.

The media arguments over dodgeball (for example, the "wussification of PE") in part focus on the quick exit and the subsequent exclusion of players who are less skilled. You can easily modify the game so that a player who is hit immediately joins the other side. Eventually, one side will have fewer and fewer players, mostly the more skilled ones, having their dodging skills tested by balls flying in from all directions.

Level II Strategies

Level II strategies promote self-motivation as an early step in the empowerment progression, including help for those who are not motivated to participate, try, or attempt new things in the activities of the lesson.

Modifying Tasks

In motor-skill instruction, rather than using teacher-directed drills you can permit students to modify their task to challenge themselves appropriately—for example, by moving closer to or farther from the basket or by setting the volleyball higher or lower (Mosston and Ashworth 1994). Although students will sometimes do this on their own, either to increase or to reduce task difficulty (if they can get away with it), building task modification into your lesson legitimizes it. By offering examples for both increasing and decreasing task difficulty in the assigned task, you facilitate students' understanding.

In fitness activities you can briefly explain the overload principle and then ask your students to overload their abdominal muscles by choosing one of three kinds of sit-ups, each at a different level of difficulty (for example, crunch, feet flat on floor, sit-down), and the number of sit-ups that will challenge them and therefore provide overload. You can use this approach with push-ups, aerobic activities (students select distance and pace, monitored by heart rate), and flexibility (students stretch to the limit of their range of motion).

By making individual commitments, your students take responsibility for pushing themselves and finding their limits. Some teachers worry that students won't push themselves, that it's the teacher's job to set goals for students and make them accomplish these goals—"We are going to do 20 push-ups" or "Pass and trap the ball back and forth until I tell you to stop." This approach can't provide an optimal challenge for all students, but more to the point, it fails to empower them. A better empowerment strategy is to make students aware that they are in charge of their bodies and that their improvement depends mostly on their commitment, their effort. Students can choose, of course, not to challenge themselves, going through the motions instead. The section "Level II: Teaching by Invitation," described in the next chapter, can help with this problem.

Self-Paced Challenges

You can implement the self-pacing strategy by sequencing physical activity tasks that have specific goals and permitting students to move at their own pace through the sequence. Some specific implementation options include the following:

- Create stations with specific goals. When an individual student completes the goal, he or she moves on to the next station.

- Create a list of gradually more difficult tasks—for example, basketball or soccer dribbling drills with increasingly more difficult obstacles and time limits. When students complete the least difficult task, they move on at their own pace through as much of the sequence as they can. A simple example, and one I've used with kids and with teachers to demonstrate self-pacing, is this progression in learning the underarm pass in volleyball:

  - Bump the ball 5 times to yourself. Do 5 in a row if you can; if you can't, do 2 plus 2 plus 1 or whatever it takes to get 5. If you are a rookie, don't hit the ball too high. If you're a pro and can control the ball, hit it to the ceiling!

  - Bump the ball 5 times to yourself off the wall, using the same guidelines. (This is more difficult than bumping in the air.)

  - Get a partner and bump the ball back and forth 10 times, again trying to do as many in a row as you can.

Form 5.1

Task Card

Modified Handball

Practice hitting the ball to the wall. Allow only one bounce after it hits the wall.

☐ I can hit the ball against the wall 5 times in a row without missing using my strong hand.

☐ I can hit the ball against the wall 10 times in a row without missing using my strong hand.

☐ I can hit the ball against the wall 5 times in a row without missing using my weak hand.

☐ I can hit the ball against the wall 10 times in a row without missing using my weak hand.

☐ I can hit the ball against the wall 10 times in a row without missing using either hand.

Adapted, by permission, from D. Hellison, 1985, Goals and strategies for teaching physical education *(Champaign, IL: Human Kinetics), 104.*

From Teaching Responsibility Through Physical Education, Second Edition *by Don Hellison, 2003, Champaign, IL: Human Kinetics.*

• Write the list of gradually more difficult tasks for different skills—for example, dribbling, passing, shooting—on task cards and place them on the wall at different stations or on individual cards that students can carry with them (in their waistband or sock) as shown in form 5.1.

You can also build task modification into these self-paced activities in a couple of ways.

• You can permit students to modify some aspect of the task—for example, by completing a certain number of successful trials but being able to adjust the distance if a target is involved or to take as many turns as they need to be successful. The previous volleyball example allows students to modify the challenge of hitting five in a row as well as to choose the height of the ball's flight.

• You can have students explore the progressions you have created and then choose either to stay with your tasks or to create and perform their own progressions in small groups.

If some students struggle with these kinds of decisions, you can give them the choice of belonging to a teacher-directed group, described in the next chapter. In a teacher-directed group, you make the decisions, not to be punitive but to provide some positive instruction for those students unwilling or incapable of making their own decisions.

Redefining Success

Losing is an important experience for all of us, but a steady diet of failure does no one any good. That's why task modification and self-paced challenges are important. A slightly different approach is to help your students redefine success for themselves so that, with sufficient effort, success is within reach. This doesn't mean eliminating the opportunity to win or lose, and it doesn't mean giving everyone awards. Redefining success means giving students options, including but not limited to the option of trying to be the best or the winner. At the same time, students must learn to respect definitions of success other than their own. The following strategies can help students redefine success:

- Improvement is one measure of success. Hand out a journal or workbook so that students can record their scores for the number of push-ups done, number of tasks completed, or even the percent of time on task. This provides self-reinforcement for their effort and progress. I've found that my inner-city kids like to write about themselves and keep track of their progress, even though for most writing is not one of their favorite activities.

- Use self-grading in which students have the opportunity to build in their own definition of success (see chapter 8 on assessment).

- Make tournaments optional, especially if they involve eliminating participants, or else offer three or four options—a competitive tournament, a less intense recreational series of games or tournament, cooperative games, or sport skill practice.

- Give individual students an out for any activity when it makes sense to do so—for example, by offering alternatives to game play such as skill drills or even a reading assignment. Forcing kids to participate is neither empowering nor motivating, and kids who have little to lose will refuse anyway.

- Create a "crazy station" for expressive activities to emphasize creativity as a legitimate personal goal. Nikos Georgiadis came up with this idea: "It proved to be a popular station, and all sorts of activities were developed, from working on Harlem Globetrotter moves to skipping and singing to a rap beat" (Williamson and Georgiadis 1992, 17).

Intensity Scale

Another empowerment strategy for participation and effort is the intensity scale. Simply ask students to privately assign themselves a number between 10 (all-out effort) and 0 (no effort) that best represents the effort that they are willing to give in a particular activity. This number can then be used in several ways:

- Give students the choice of joining one of three or four activity groups, each of which has a designated maximum and minimum intensity—for example, 8–10, 4–7, and 1–3 groups. This method will bring together kids willing to expend similar effort, reducing conflict over students who "don't try" or "don't want to win" and providing a more supportive environment in all groups.

- Ask students to compare their number to the minimum required for game participation—in the preceding example 8, 4, or 1—to determine whether to participate. In the process, students learn that group activities require a certain effort because others depend on them, whereas giving little effort in an individual task affects only the individual.

- After the activity, ask students to evaluate their actual effort and compare that number to their preparticipation prediction. By reflecting, students begin to learn to predict more accurately. For example, many students don't feel motivated until they begin to participate.

Level III Strategies

An empowerment progression does not honor clean divisions such as Level II and Level III. Lines blur because your students (and you) are human! Most of us develop in fits and starts with plenty of backsliding. The levels are an artificial construct intended to facilitate, not handcuff, a complex process that is further complicated by individual differences.

Having acknowledged that, the empowerment theme is expressed in Level I mostly as negotiation (see the next chapter), whereas Level II strategies provide limited decision-making opportunities. Level III strategies further expand individual decision making. To experience self-direction fully, students eventually need the opportunity to create and carry out a personal plan that addresses their needs (that is, a plan for development or improvement) and interests (for example, having fun, being with friends). Your kids may not be able to do this yet, but at least they ought to be aware of the existence of an empowerment progression that leads to having a personal plan.

You might use yourself as an example by sharing your personal plan, especially the physical activity dimension and perhaps even a plan to improve a personal or social skill. (Doing that will also make you more human in the eyes of your kids!)

The next chapter addresses problems that students have with Level III.

On-Task Independence

The first step toward on-task independence is having students do independent work assigned by you without direct supervision—for example, offering independent station work in which you choose the tasks. You can then progress to having students choose from several stations with different tasks, depending on the student's evaluation of her or his needs and interests. To facilitate this step, briefly talk to your students about how to assess their own needs and interests as the basis for making choices.

The following fitness example, which I've used with students from seventh grade through high school, describes more specifically one way to get started in promoting on-task independence:

1. Start with a 10- to 15-minute (adjusted to your situation) fitness routine directed by you. Integrate fitness concepts such as overload and aerobic activity into the routine so that the students' knowledge base becomes sufficient for making a Level III personal plan.

2. On a day when they seem ready, ask students to do the fitness routine on their own and at their own pace. Those who can't or won't need to join your teacher-directed group. Most just need a reminder or some encouragement. If necessary, post the routine to remind students.

3. Permit students to develop their own fitness routine for the 10- to 15-minute fitness period. They can reorder the exercises, skip those they don't like, or even spend the entire time on jogging or some other fitness activity if they choose. The rationale is that by this time students know the fitness concepts and have had some positive experiences. If a few still don't see the benefit or don't like some of the activities, that is their choice. Someone usually asks, "Can we spend the entire time stretching?" "Sure," I respond, "as long as you do stretching and not just talking." Just stretching quickly becomes boring for most students.

Goal-Setting Progression

The last step in the preceding fitness-progression example involves goal setting (rather than on-task independence). As students extend the progression—whether in fitness, motor skills, or something else—they can take on more responsibility for developing personal plans based on their goals. Eventually they can come up with ways to evaluate themselves, such as amount of time it takes to accomplish a specific task related to their goal, number of times they can accomplish a specific task compared to their last self-test, or improvement in their mechanics based on the input of someone who knows the correct cues.

Goal setting, as suggested in chapter 3, will depend on your kids' ages, self-motivation, and an understanding of the goal-setting process.

- Make sure that your students know what a goal is.
- You can set goals for students until they get the idea, but the goal needs to be important to them or they won't work on it on their own.
- Set goals that are under the student's control and realistic—outdoing others, for example, is not fully within an individual's grasp, whereas improving one's percentage of free throws is likely to be so.
- Goals should be measurable, whether quantitatively (by counting) or qualitatively (by description).
- Goals should be short term at first, then gradually extended to long term.
- Students need to receive feedback on their progress. One way is to help them keep track of their progress, whether using quantitative or qualitative evaluation. You can also give feedback to individual students, as can student leaders if you teach them how. You can use some version of reciprocal coaching as described under Level IV strategies to get peers involved as well.
- With your help students need to establish and practice strategies to achieve their goals. Eventually, they should be able to make and carry out a personal physical activity plan.

For more information, see chapter 9 by Tom Martinek in Hellison et al. (2000) and Weinberg and Gould (1999).

One way to help students set goals is the self-report shown in form 5.2. I have used this self-report expanded to include motor-skill development in order to help my students set goals.

To set, carry out, and evaluate personal goals, students need self-knowledge and conceptual knowledge. Students must understand fitness concepts if they are to plan their own fitness programs. If motor skill improvement is their goal, they must grasp and apply motor-learning concepts such as practice and feedback. Teaching

Form 5.2

Self-Report

Name _____

Desire to improve

Body fat: I have

___ too much   Yes   No   Don't care

___ enough

___ too little

Cardiovascular endurance: I can

___ run 2 miles in 12 min   Yes   No   Don't care

___ jog a mile

___ get out of breath easily

Flexibility: I can

___ touch my toes easily   Yes   No   Don't care

___ touch my toes barely

___ not reach my toes

___ not reach much beyond my knees

Relaxation: I can

___ never seem to relax   Yes   No   Don't care

___ relax sometimes

___ relax whenever I want to

Strength: I am

___ very strong   Yes   No   Don't care

___ strong enough to take care of myself
in an emergency

___ too weak to take care of myself in an
emergency

Speed: I can run away from trouble

___ if my assailants have broken legs   Yes   No   Don't care

___ in some situations

___ usually

___ almost always   **(continued)**

Form 5.2 *(continued)*

Self-Report

Desire to improve

Self-defense: My self-defense skills are good
enough to

___ get me in deep trouble   Yes No Don't care

___ help me a little bit

___ help me in most situations

___ help me in any situation I can imagine

Water safety: I can swim, float, and tread
water for

___ over an hour   Yes No Don't care

___ over 30 min

___ at least 15 min

___ glub-glub

My body is:

___ muscular   ___ heavy   Yes No Don't care

___ soft   ___ just right

                ___ light

My posture is:

___ poor   Yes No Don't care

___ average

___ good

Adapted, by permission, from D. Hellison, 1985, Goals and strategies for
teaching physical education, *(Champaign, IL: Human Kinetics),* 90-92.

From Teaching Responsibility Through Physical Education,
Second Edition by Don Hellison, 2003, Champaign, IL: Human Kinetics.

basic concepts simultaneously with fitness and skill instruction helps
prepare students for Level III time. If students know that they must
understand the basic concepts before they can work on their own, it
is my experience that they'll learn them!

Personal Plan

Students can progress to developing their own personal plan, again
by taking a step at a time. A personal plan can take a variety of forms,

Form 5.3

Checklist of My Personal Goals for Today

Do three of these activities. Check them off, fill in how many you did, and hand this form in to me. I will announce the activity at the instructional station. If you want to do it, come to this station first.

___ Flexibility exercises: How many different stretches did you do? ___

___ Push-ups: How many? ___

___ Laps: How many? ___ 6-second pulse rate ___

___ Ten free throw attempts: How many baskets? ___

___ Ten jump shot attempts from same spot: How many baskets? ___

___ Ten volleyball bumps to self: How many in a row? ___

___ Ten volleyball sets off the wall: How many in a row? ___

___ Volleyball sets and bumps in a row with a partner (three tries): How many? ___

___ Ten soccer passes against the wall: How many in a row? ___

___ Crazy station (any creative activity with or without equipment): What did you do? _____

___ Instructional station (see me): What did you learn? _____

_____

_____

depending on the developmental level of individual students, class size, and the amount of paperwork you can tolerate. The plan can take several forms:

- Checklists (see form 5.3 for a sample)
- Oral contracts (a student who told me, "I need to work on shooting and not laughing at others," made progress in both areas without anything other than a reminder here and there)
- Written contracts, or records as illustrated in form 5.4 and form 5.5
- Workbook entries

Once you introduce Level III (or self-direction) time, you ought to schedule it regularly for those who can handle it. This time can be

Form 5.4

My Personal Plan #1

1. Fitness: Choose at least one

   My flexibility goal is _____.

   My strength goal is _____.

   My aerobic goal is _____.

   Today in fitness I did _____.

2. Motor skills: Choose at least one skill from one activity

   My basketball goal is _____.

   My volleyball goal is _____.

   My soccer goal is _____.

   My _____ goal is _____.

   Today in motor skill development I did _____.

3. Choose one

   The creative/expressive activity I did was _____.

   I spent my "pal time" with _____ doing _____.

   The stress management activity I did today was_____.

   The self-defense activity I did today was _____.

4. During my Level III time

   My respect for others was

   ___ good   ___ OK   ___ not OK

   My effort was

   ___ high   ___ medium   ___ low

   My plan was

   ___ my own   ___ somewhat my own   ___ not my own

   My self-discipline in carrying out my plan was

   ___ good   ___ fair   ___ poor

   I helped someone else.

   ___ Yes!   ___ A little   ___ No!

From Teaching Responsibility Through Physical Education,
Second Edition by Don Hellison, 2003, Champaign, IL: Human Kinetics.

Form 5.5

My Personal Plan #2

The first 15 minutes

My goal:

What I will be doing:

How I will measure my progress:

The second 15 minutes

My goal:

What I will be doing:

How I will measure my progress:

From Teaching Responsibility Through Physical Education,
Second Edition *by Don Hellison, 2003, Champaign, IL: Human Kinetics.*

brief at first but you should lengthen it as students improve their knowledge base and become more proficient at working on their own, setting goals, and evaluating their progress. If you offer Level III time sporadically, it may not make much of a contribution to the development of self-direction. If you do suspend Level III time, be sure your students know why.

Level III for Children?

As with everything, Level III challenges need to be developmentally appropriate. Even first graders have demonstrated considerable responsibility on occasion—for example, by making and carrying out written Level III contracts in one school and planning a curriculum unit in another. Of course, older students can take on more responsibility. However, children can often do more than we expect of them, and older youth are, as one eighth grader told me, "Pretty set in our ways," which may make them less open to innovative teaching strategies. You can tiptoe into Level III with little kids, but give them the chance to spread their wings a bit. Have a little faith in them, and you might be surprised at the result. Alfie Kohn (1993, 14) gave this advice:

> It goes without saying that a 16-year-old can approach a decision in a more sophisticated way than a 6-year-old and therefore can usually be entrusted with more responsibility. But this fact is sometimes used to justify preventing younger children from making choices that are well within their capabilities. Moreover, the idea that we must wait until the children are mature enough to handle responsibilities may set up a vicious circle; after all, it is experience with decision-making that helps children become capable of handling them.

LEVEL IV STRATEGIES

Walt Kelly, football coach and high school PE teacher in Bozeman, Montana, tells his students that for all games there is one primary rule: Be at Level IV. That means they must cooperate, be trustworthy, support each other, help each other, and assume their share of leadership (thanks to Walt for this example).

Helping and Leadership Roles

To promote Level IV experiences, you can integrate helping roles into the lesson. Reciprocal coaching (adapted from Mosston and Ashworth 1994) gives every student a chance to learn how to give appropriate feedback to a peer when both are practicing a specific motor skill. One of a pair of students is temporarily assigned to be the coach, which means that he or she observes the other student in relation to three specific cues (for example, kick with the shoelaces, not the toe). After a few turns they switch roles. When both have taken their turns, they get together and share how well the other person coached them. Did the other student say anything? Was the other person positive? Was the person helpful? Note that they talk about their performance as coaches, not as players. You need to set up this strategy carefully to ensure that students know the relevant cues and give positive feedback.

Peer teaching and coaching roles offer students advanced experiences at Level IV. Traditionally, assigned roles were limited to leading an exercise routine familiar to the students in class, and those chosen were usually athletes or the more highly skilled kids. Being a good athlete isn't enough. It may help, especially in coaching, if the student leader brings to the experience relevant sport knowledge or if kids have high regard for those who are athletes or highly skilled. But it isn't necessary. What is necessary, depending on the developmental level of your class, is at least some beginning sign of

- caring and compassion, which refers to the student leader's intrinsic interest in helping a peer, in truly caring about his or her well-being and development;
- sensitivity and responsiveness, which refers to the program leader's ability to size up what other students need and can handle, and being responsive to these needs; and
- inner strength, which is necessary because leaders' decisions and actions will not always be popular. For example, leaders need to be able to confront kids who are fooling around and get them to focus.

Although these criteria are not precisely measurable (which is often the case with the qualities we most prize), you need to inform all your students about what it takes to become a successful leader. Doing this serves the purposes of

- making it clear that everyone, not just the physically elite kids, can work at becoming a leader;
- helping teach students what Level IV is really all about; and
- positively reinforcing these qualities in chosen leaders.

Students can provide leadership during skill drills and fitness exercises, first by following your instructions and later, after you give them the responsibility, by making some decisions about what and how to teach. You can call the leaders together to give them their instructions while the other students have a brief free play period (or some activity they can do without instruction such as walking and running around the perimeter of the gym). You can also write instructions for the leaders on a card so that they will have reminders or prompts during their leadership experience, as Jay Nacu does for his martial-arts program with fourth through eighth graders (see form 5.6). These leadership meetings will take more time at first but much less later on. Eventually, handing them a card may be enough to get them started, and as they acquire experience and begin making some decisions, they won't even need that.

Form 5.6

Front kick with back leg
- Left foot forward fighting stance
- Keep your guard up
- Front knee bent
- Back leg comes up in front with knee to chest
- Extend kicking leg
- Kick with ball-of-foot/toes
- Snap back kicking leg
- Step back with kicking leg

Do the same with right leg forward

Roundhouse kick with back leg
- Left foot forward fighting stance
- Keep your guard up
- Front knee bent
- Back leg comes up to the side
- Pivot on front foot
- Extend kicking leg
- Kick with shoelaces/instep
- Snap back kicking leg
- Step back with kicking leg

Do the same with right leg forward

Side kick with back leg
- Left foot forward fighting stance
- Keep your guard up
- Front knee bent
- Back leg comes up in front with knee to chest
- Pivot on stationary foot
- Extend kicking leg
- Kick with side edge of foot
- Snap back kicking leg
- Step back with kicking leg

Do the same with right leg forward

Jab-cross combination
- Left foot forward fighting stance
- Keep your guard up
- Front knee bent
- Lead hand extends with a fist
- Back hand extends with a fist while pivoting off the back foot

Do the same with right leg forward

From Teaching Responsibility Through Physical Education,
Second Edition *by Don Hellison, 2003, Champaign, IL: Human Kinetics.*

Front kick with front leg: jab kick
- Left foot forward fighting stance
- Keep your guard up
- Front knee bent
- Shift weight to back leg
- Front leg comes up in front with knee to chest
- Extend kicking leg
- Kick with ball-of-foot/toes
- Snap back kicking leg
- Step down with kicking leg

Do the same with right leg forward

Roundhouse kick with front leg
- Left foot forward fighting stance
- Keep your guard up
- Front knee bent
- Shift weight to back leg
- Front leg comes up
- Pivot on back foot
- Extend kicking leg
- Kick with shoelaces/instep
- Snap back kicking leg
- Step down with kicking leg

Do the same with right leg forward

Side kick stepping behind front foot
- Left foot forward fighting stance
- Keep your guard up
- Front knee bent
- Back foot steps behind front foot
- Front leg comes up in front with knee to chest
- Extend kicking leg
- Kick with side edge of foot
- Snap back kicking leg
- Kicking leg comes down
- Step back with back leg

Do the same with right leg forward

From Jay Nacu with permission.

From Teaching Responsibility Through Physical Education,
Second Edition *by Don Hellison, 2003, Champaign, IL: Human Kinetics.*

Students can also assume coaching roles during game practice and play, as popularized by sport education (Siedentop 1994). Again, you will need to develop a progression beginning with specific instructions for the practice (for example, drills, offensive

KidQuotes

"We were fabulous. We passed the ball all around and didn't get an attitude."—Sixth grader

"I need to work on my shooting and on not laughing at others."—Eighth grader

"We drew up an obstacle course; now we want to set it up and teach it to everyone."—Seventh grader

plays, defensive formations) supplemented by cards (which become "coaching cards") to give prompts to coaches. The practice can be scripted, at least at first, but leadership in a game is much more fluid and therefore more difficult.

Although I support teachers who use sport education, TPSR requires some different rules and procedures for game play. For example, self-officiating is necessary rather than assigning a referee because the presence of a referee takes that responsibility away from the players, leaving them just to avoid being caught. (See the conflict resolution section in chapter 6 for more about this.) One way coaches can show leadership is by calling time-outs to solve foul-calling or offensive/defensive problems or conflict issues. Nikos Georgiadis developed a strategy based on the two-tier system of time-outs used in professional basketball (NBA) whereby student coaches can call either a 20-second time-out (by touching the shoulders) for small problems or a full time-out (by making a T with their hands) for big problems, whether the sport is basketball or something else (thanks to Nikos for this example). Although the coaches are in charge, anyone can call a time-out at any time during any game, as long as he or she does not abuse the privilege. To help students get the idea, you can call the time-outs at first and take the lead in helping students solve problems. At the same time you explain that they have the right and the responsibility to solve these problems, but they have to call time-outs to do so. Before every game I tell coaches that if I have to step in, they aren't doing their jobs. Some fourth graders have shown the ability to call time-outs in my programs and have enough skill to handle team meetings. Eventually student coaches may be able to head off such problems as angry outbursts, verbal abuse, and low motivation by noticing the first signs of trouble.

You can also assign assistant leader and coach roles for students who demonstrate some of the necessary leadership qualities but aren't quite ready to assume a leader or coach role. Assistants should have one specific leadership task assigned to them, for example, running one specific drill in practice (thanks to Dave Walsh).

Tom Martinek (Veal, Ennis, Hellison, Martinek, and O'Sullivan 2002) uses this helping-leadership progression:

1. Helping someone one on one
2. Providing leadership for a few students
3. Coaching a team in class
4. Teaching new students in class the levels and class procedures
5. Cross-age teaching

Group Goals

Nikos Georgiadis, a youth work professional, and Bobby Lifka, a middle school PE teacher, have used group goals to promote Level IV experience. In this strategy, students are divided into small groups that decide on a group goal for the activity—for example, number of sit-ups, amount of rope-skipping time, or number of volleyball sets off the wall. Then the students attempt to attain their group goal, contributing what they can. The point is to have each student contribute to the group effort. In rope skipping, for example, if the group sets a 3-minute goal, at least one person in the group needs to be skipping rope at all times during the 3-minute period. If the goal is 60 sit-ups, group members do what they can, and then each volunteers to do more until the group reaches the goal (thanks to Nikos and Bobby for this idea).

Giraffe Club

I have never done this, but creating a Giraffe Club for those "who stick their necks out for the common good" has been used to reinforce elementary school children who have demonstrated Level IV on a regular basis (Lickona 1991, 309). The presence of a Giraffe Club focuses attention on the value of Level IV and those students who practice it. To add a group-empowerment dimension to this strategy, students can participate in the selection of Giraffes. They can also be included in conversations about the benefits and drawbacks of starting a Giraffe Club.

LEVEL V STRATEGIES

Although Level V is intended to focus students' attention on becoming responsible outside the gym, in-class cross-age teaching and service projects do promote Level V involvement. Cross-age teaching, where experienced student leaders teach small groups of younger children what they have learned, is a powerful Level IV–Level V experience (Level V because they are providing a service to the school beyond typical PE class experiences). My eighth-grade and high school students have demonstrated the ability to conduct awareness talks, a lesson, a group meeting, and reflection time with 10-year-olds. There are at least two ways to do this. You can have your students practice teaching with each other, sort of a mini-student-teaching experience (try using video so that they can see themselves teach), followed by a one-shot teaching experience with an invited class of younger children. I've done this a number of times, and even when they had only one experience teaching a group of younger kids, they talked about being teachers after class, reflecting at least a fleeting glimmer of Level V as well as the impression Level IV made on them. My more successful cross-age teaching experiences, as well as those of Tom Martinek, have been daily or weekly commitments to provide cross-age leadership with the same kids for a semester. Nick Cutforth has had success inviting former class members who had graduated to middle school to come back and provide leadership in their former class (Hellison et al. 2000).

Any service project the group takes on that attempts to make a social contribution qualifies as Level IV experience. Recently, a group of seventh- and eighth-grade students made a martial-arts video that promoted self-control and nonviolence, and they showed it to administrators and other students in the school (thanks to Stein Garcia).

The strategies in this chapter are intended to help you integrate TPSR into your physical activity lesson. During the lesson, however, problems and situations arise that these strategies do not address. The next chapter does.

Take-Aways

Here are some things from this chapter that you might consider taking with you:

- Integration of responsibility-based strategies into the physical activity lesson is perhaps the most difficult aspect of TPSR implementation.
- By using a strategy progression, you can tiptoe into integration, gradually moving from direct instruction and awareness talks to more individual and group empowerment—from smaller voices and choices (with reflection) to larger voices and choices (thanks to Bobby Lifka).

- Each level, including Level V, has a range of possible strategies. Your job is to select and adapt these strategies for your situation and kids.
- Younger kids are not exempt from the empowerment process, although you need to modify the process so that it is developmentally appropriate.

Chapter 6

STRATEGIES FOR SPECIFIC PROBLEMS AND SITUATIONS

Discipline is not a matter of keeping things under control by making choices for students . . . it is a matter of helping students learn to make good choices and to be responsible for those choices. —Peggy Pastor

Having a purpose, some curricular goals and themes, and a lesson-plan format that represent your beliefs and values as a teacher provides guidelines for your everyday practice. But what happens when you're confronted with something unplanned, a surprising and unusual problem or situation? Even with something you've faced before, the solution you used the first time may not work again. Three general strategies can help:

- self-reflection (Hellison and Templin 1991);
- reflection-in-action (Schon 1987), including a solutions bank (Orlick 1980); and
- fattening your bag of tricks.

SELF-REFLECTION AND REFLECTION-IN-ACTION

Self-reflection should be part of a teacher's bag of tricks and present in all of one's teaching practice, especially so in TPSR. Reflection-in-action is a special form of self-reflection.

Self-Reflection

Self-reflection is central to planning, carrying out, and evaluating your lessons. Two overriding questions can guide you:

1. "What's worth doing in my professional life?" This question is about the heart and soul of your practice—your convictions and sense of purpose. Whether what you're doing is working well or not, is it the kind of contribution you want to make?

2. "Is it working?" Or more appropriately, what ideas and strategies are working, which ones aren't, and why or why not? What do you need to do to improve your practice?

Self-reflection is particularly useful after a day of teaching, that is, if you have any energy left to do it. Keeping a journal formalizes the process and may provide you with a small measure of accountability. Reflecting on how you handled unplanned problems and situations that arose that day and what might have worked better sharpens your ability to solve problems and therefore improve your teaching practice. You begin to accumulate experience in reflective problem solving, in thinking about alternative ways of dealing with the wide variety of issues that teachers face in today's world. In the process, you fatten your bag of tricks.

Howe (1991) derived an important insight from his ability to reflect on his experiences with hostile at-risk kids:

> A lot of horseplay . . . verges on a full-fledged fight, but seldom becomes one. . . . [Students] take their stand and then allow one another to back down with dignity (p. 24). . . . They do not really want to get hurt, so if they must provoke a fight, they will choose the most protective environment, which is the school (p. 30).

Self-Assessment

Although assessment has usurped center stage in education in many states, self-assessment is closely aligned with self-reflection, as Camino (2002, 40) made clear:

- Self-assessment is a process of discovery.
- Self-assessment should lead to reflection and discussion, and then to action—otherwise it is an empty exercise.
- Self-assessment and continuous improvement are not one-time occurrences. Each is an ongoing process—strengthening what works or is promising, stopping what doesn't, and making information-based decisions that both youth and adults have contributed to.

Reflection-in-Action

Reflection-in-action is a much less contemplative process than self-reflection and self-assessment; it's more like making a snap judgment of what to do now based on a quick analysis of the situation. Even if you've faced the same situation before, the problem may well require a different solution. Schon (1987, 26) argued that reflection-in-action is different from knowing-in-action.

> [Knowing-in-action means we] have learned how to do something, we can execute smooth sequences of activity, recognition, decision, and adjustment without having, as we say, to "think about it." . . . [Reflection-in-action, on the other hand, refers to a brief period of time] during which we can still make a difference to the situation at hand—our thinking serves to reshape what we are doing while we are doing it.

Schon described reflection-in-action as beginning with a surprise, something unexpected, which leads to questioning the assumptions of knowing-in-action and culminates in an on-the-spot experiment. Reflective problem solving—for example, by keeping a self-reflection journal as described earlier—can help you develop reflection-in-action skills. Solution banks can also be helpful.

Solution Banks

A solution bank is an example of using self-reflection before the lesson rather than after, as in keeping a journal. Learning to prepare lesson plans is a staple of teacher education programs, but preservice teachers rarely gain sufficient experience in preparing solution banks. A solution bank is simply a list of ifs and thens—as in "if such-and-such happens, then I'll try this." For example, if two students start screaming at each other while tempers soar, you might write down "I'll separate them, let them cool down, and then get them together to get the issue handled or dropped." The point is not that your strategy will always work; nothing always works! Instead, thinking about possible problems and situations as well as possible solutions mentally prepares you for these occurrences. It is a warm-up, a practice session, for reflection-in-action in your classes. If you are unprepared, your only choice is to react spontaneously—to shoot from the hip—and hope for the best.

FATTENING YOUR BAG OF TRICKS

Developing your skill at reflection-in-action as well as self-reflection of your teaching practice in general can help you deal more effectively with problems and situations that crop up from time to time. Although these general approaches are useful, having some TPSR strategies for specific scenarios in your bag of tricks will further prepare you for teaching responsibility in tough situations.

Level I: Individual Discipline Problems

The discipline policy of elementary school principal Peggy Pastor (2002, 659) could easily have been written for TPSR:

> What is it about schools that takes responsibility away from our students and brings many of them to an "us against them" attitude by the time they reach high school? . . . Discipline is not a matter of keeping things under control by making choices for students . . . it is a matter of helping students learn to make good choices and to be responsible for those choices. . . . [Although] we no longer believe that all children learn to read in the same way . . . in matters of . . . discipline we still seem to think and act as if one size fits all.

Pastor told the story of Robby, who was referred to her countless times for fighting on the playground. Nothing seemed to work, so she told him that she wanted to help him but didn't know how. He offered to help and came up with several ideas, some of which he immediately rejected as he talked but three of which he thought might work. He picked one and wrote it down. They both signed it, and Robby—although he was still a difficult child in a number of ways—never again got into a fight on the playground.

Despite the work of Pastor and others, "Teachers tend to think of discipline dichotomously, as being either authoritarian or permissive, and to think of being democratic as being permissive" (Power 2002, 135). The TPSR version of responsibility is neither "Do what I say and you're being responsible" nor "Do whatever you please." It walks the fine line between personal choice and social-moral responsibility, relying on dialog, self-reflection, accountability, and the "logical consequences" described by Dreikurs and Soltz (1964).

Applying the Accordion Principle Effectively

Many Level I problems happen during game play, although any situation from standing in line to doing fitness activities is fair game for disruption and abuse. A common strategy is to expand and reduce time allotted for game play in relation to the amount of abusive and disruptive behavior. This is an example of the accordion principle, and although it certainly sounds like behavior modification, it is also an example of using a logical consequence to teach responsible participation (Dreikurs and Soltz 1964). If you apply it to the whole class, however, you also penalize those who aren't causing problems. For them, losing game time is definitely not a logical consequence of their actions. In most circumstances a more equitable method is to apply the accordion principle individually so that only those who are causing the problems experience the logical consequence of reduced game play (or whatever activity they are engaged in).

Sit-Out Progression

The sit-out progression is designed for kids who "get an attitude," lose their temper, or argue a lot. These attitudes and behaviors most commonly emerge during game play, although they do occur elsewhere as well (and the same strategies apply). Wherever they occur, negotiation, a key component of the empowerment theme, must be built in to the sit-out progression. In brief, this progression involves

1. the choice of sitting out or getting under control (not abusive),
2. sitting out with the choice of returning when ready to put Level I into practice,
3. sitting out until you and the student can negotiate a plan,
4. renegotiating a different plan, and
5. referring the student for special help.

In the first step, sitting out can be treated as a choice if the incident is not violent. When my students put on a "mean face" to show their anger, I ask them to change their face or have a seat until they can do so. You can handle many incidents this way unless the disrespect is flagrant or the same problem occurs repeatedly (which means that the sit-out option didn't work). When confronted with the option, some students choose to sit out for several minutes, even when playing their beloved game of basketball, but many students will never choose to sit out. If they choose not to sit out and fail to change their disruptive or abusive behavior, you can tell them to sit out whether they want to or not, but they can come back in on their own when they can participate responsibly. Note that even at this stage they still have a choice of coming back in whenever they are ready. If this doesn't work, tell them to stay seated until you can join them to negotiate some kind of Level I plan. The steps for negotiating this plan (Glasser 1965, 1977; Raffini 1980) are as follows:

1. Agree on the problem and the student's role in it. Level I problems of self-control such as intimidating or making fun of others or losing one's temper are often compounded by blaming others or in some cases totally denying the behavior. If possible, try to get the student to understand that he or she harmed or caused a problem for someone else. Agreeing on the problem may take some work and some listening by both you and the student. Others may be implicated during this process, but

try to focus on the student's role. If you cannot reach an agreement, for example, if the student denies any involvement even though clearly implicated, move on to step two anyway.

2. Negotiate and agree on a plan to solve the problem. Any plan that addresses the problem and doesn't cause a new problem for someone else is OK. If the student won't participate in this process (which is common if the problem has not been agreed upon), suggest some plans and attempt to get the student to agree to one. I will often suggest some kind of restitution if abuse toward other students is involved. It is amazing how quickly students come up with an alternative plan if they don't like mine!

3. Follow up to make sure the student complies with the plan. The plan may need to be in writing. Without follow-through, the process breaks down.

4. If the student does not follow the plan, make a new and different plan. Don't repeat a plan that hasn't worked. Glasser (1977) suggested using progressive separation from the group, meaning that plans need to begin to isolate the student from those who are being harmed by the student's actions. This does not necessarily mean sitting out; for example, a student can still do fitness exercises or some sport skill drills alone at a station.

5. As a last resort, refer the student for special help. Students should have a right of exit from a program that doesn't work for them or for the rest of the class with them in it.

"No plan, no play" is a shorthand variation of the sit-out progression (DeLine 1991). The student is not allowed back into the game unless he or she comes up with a plan to change the behavior that resulted in the suspension. The "no plan, no play" strategy can also be used when two students are involved (see "Level I: Conflict Resolution Strategies," p. 88).

This process, like everything else in this book, is only a suggestion. It gives you guidance by providing specific steps. But you may not have the time to do all these steps, or they may be inappropriate for the situation. The key, based on the TPSR themes of empowerment and teacher-student interaction, is to involve students as much as possible in the process. Involvement will vary from student to student and from meeting to meeting, but the goal is always the same: to give students a say in their life in the gym.

Grandma's Law

If students display disinterest in or disdain for an activity you have introduced, you may need to resort to grandma's (or grandpa's) law.

Grandma's law states that one must eat one's dinner before going out to play. Although it is important to listen to students' feelings about having to do the activity, a mandatory introductory experience free of expressions of distaste often wins kids over. I've experienced this several times, most recently in volleyball—"That's for girls," the boys told me. They were in no mood for a group meeting, so I just used grandma's law spontaneously: "If we can do volleyball without griping, we'll do basketball afterward." Within a month they were choosing to play volleyball! I also used it in teaching yoga followed by basketball, but without the same level of success. They did the yoga without protest, but only one student chose to do yoga when given a choice.

Teacher-Directed Group

One way to handle problems of disruption and abuse (Level I), which also works for students not motivated to participate (Level II) or unwilling or unable to work on their own (Level III), is to create two groups, a teacher-directed group and a self-directed group, whenever you give students some responsibility—for example, during station work. This strategy meets the need of teachers who want to individualize but can't figure out a way to do so. Of course, you can build this strategy into your curriculum-instruction plan, but that assumes that some kids will need such a group. Although that may be true, I prefer to envision it as a response to the need for more supervision of some of the class. That way, I stay positive about all the kids (at least for a while), and dip into my bag of tricks for the teacher-directed group strategy only when necessary.

Jeff Walsh, a Portland, Oregon, middle school teacher, gave his students a choice of three activity stations—for example, weightlifting, volleyball, or soccer. But students who were disruptive, abusive, or off task joined a teacher-directed group and followed Jeff as he went from station to station. He stopped activity at each station to teach a minilesson, and the teacher-directed group became students at this station. To graduate to the self-directed group and thereby be able to choose one station, students had to demonstrate that they could function at Levels I, II, and III (or Level III in the cumulative levels) (thanks to Jeff for this example).

Five Clean Days

As a last resort, you could institute a strategy requiring students to complete five clean days, as I did in my early years after several weeks of frustration in my attempts to introduce TPSR to my inner-city high school PE students (Hellison 1978). Students could earn the right to devise and carry out a personal plan for a day if they successfully completed five days in a row at Levels I and II. (Of course, it could be any number of days; we met daily, so a week of clean days made sense.) By experiencing Levels I and II, they earned Level III. At first, Level III was simple: Be on task in an activity of your choice (providing space was available). Soon, however, it was evident that they could take much more responsibility. They wrote and put into practice detailed contracts, eventually including an evaluation plan. This is behavior modification, but as in the other behavior modification strategies, a logical consequence—permission to make some choices and work on one's own—was a consequence of being under control and motivated to participate. To move away from this system, I used open negotiation in the second semester, which permitted all students to make and implement a personal plan provided they kept a record of their work and negotiated all Level I, II, and III problems with me.

Referral

Does everyone live happily ever after if you do all these things? If you have been teaching for any length of time, you already know the answer to that. Some kids come to you on medication or having experienced inappropriate prenatal care or dealing with any of a hundred other problems. You'll never reach all of these kids; maybe someone else will, maybe not. Perhaps most frustrating are those students who harm others and show no remorse. These young people are usually hard-core cases who require long-term specialized counseling if they are to have a chance of avoiding the juvenile or adult justice system and becoming a positive member of society. Despite weak referral systems in many schools, a few students should have the right of exit from programs that just don't work for them and whose presence reduces the effectiveness of the program for others. They need special help, and it would best serve them, their PE class, and you if they got that help.

Level I: Conflict Resolution Strategies

Sometimes, you can negotiate conflicts during the group meeting, but often it is difficult to solve an issue with the whole class chiming in. Additionally, many conflicts are potentially too volatile to negotiate in that setting.

Sport Court

When issues come up in class or in the group meeting, individuals can make suggestions, and sometimes a show of hands will resolve the issue, but if the problem requires extended discussion, a small group may be able to discuss it and come to a decision more easily.

Of course, you can step in and make the decision after receiving student input, but sometimes the issue is so controversial that referral to a student committee seems more appropriate. A sport court consists of three students elected by the students to make decisions on disputes that the group cannot come to agreement on. In one program serving 6- to 17-year-olds labeled as severely emotionally disturbed, the sport court seemed to function swiftly, fairly, and effectively. You could hear a pin drop when they announced their verdict, which was routinely tougher than what I would have done.

Self-Officiating

In games the job of officials is to ensure that players follow the rules and to resolve disputes. Self-officiating places responsibility on students to resolve conflicts themselves rather than just trying to avoid being caught by an official. But monitoring oneself and pointing out one's own mistakes are no easy tasks for most kids. Struggling through this process, while time-consuming and sometimes rancorous, does teach kids how to solve conflicts. Who last touched the ball? Was she safe or out? Was there a foul on that play? These aren't world-changing issues, but they matter to the players. My rules are simple:

- Assigned student leaders, captains, or coaches have the lead responsibility, but everyone is part of the process.
- Get it handled!
- Do it without anger or disrespect.
- Listen to all sides.
- If I have to get involved, you are not being responsible (especially coaches or captains if designated).

Don Andersen, an elementary school PE teacher in the Chicago area, has adopted this policy: He doesn't officiate, but if he sees a student commit an obvious rule violation and the student does not make the call, that student is required to give up the ball and sit out for 30 seconds, leaving the team shorthanded. It's behavior modification, but it is at least partly a logical consequence of failing to call a rules violation on oneself. It is also a wakeup call to start self-officiating (thanks to Don for this example).

Talking Bench

The talking-bench strategy addresses the conflict resolution component of Level I (Horrocks 1978). To resolve a conflict between two students, the teacher asks the involved students to go to an area, such as a bench, designated for talking. They resolve the problem and report back to the teacher that the problem is resolved (perhaps by saying, "It's over") before returning to the activity. As in other conflicts, the rules are show respect, listen to both sides, and resolve it. One teacher requires students to "come up with one story of what happened" (Lickona 1991, 296). You may need to help in this process, but you cannot act as a referee, which would remove responsibility from the students for solving their problem. Mike DeBusk reported hearing the conversation of two fourth-grade boys who were heading for the talking bench. One said, "Let's tell him it's over," and the other agreed. They pivoted and came back to Mike, told him they had handled it, and he said OK. As he explained, they did handle it (thanks to Mike for this example)!

Emergency Plan

California elementary physical education teacher Rudy Benton's idea of creating an emergency plan at a group meeting before games empowers students to determine a generic method for handling conflicts during the game. The group may decide, for example, to flip a coin to decide disputes. When a dispute arises, however, students are often reluctant to put their emergency plan into practice; they would rather argue! Reminders help.

Making New Rules

A variation of the emergency plan is to ask students to make rules to handle the problems they are having. You can also use this technique to head off Level I problems by asking students to make "respect rules." They know how they would like to be treated; have them share these things and then create some rules for class.

Conflicts sometimes occur at stations where a handful of students are involved in doing task sheets, a drill, a team practice, a game, or some other activity. A challenging example from my experience involved a trampoline station (it's an old story!), where serious safety considerations as well as issues surrounding taking turns and the length of a turn caused one problem after another. I reminded the students about using the levels in resolving problems. Still they complained incessantly. I required that they make station rules. The rules they made didn't work, so they made new rules. And additional new rules. Then they requested that I police them. I did that for a little while and then asked them to try again. They got better—safer, happier—but it was gradual progress with considerable backsliding.

Level II: Teaching by Invitation

The Level II strategies described in the last chapter are designed to promote self-motivation and extend the empowerment process begun with negotiation at Level I. But experiencing a new activity or one in which some students have had little success in the past may have to begin with an invitation to these individual students to "go through the motions." For example, in fitness activities I have invited reluctant participants to "just try a couple of sit-ups" or "just walk" to get them started. I accompany the invitation with a description of what they need to do to get some benefit out of the activity. I also state my belief that effort is the first step in taking personal responsibility. Another invitation that I've had some success with is to say, "Try it my way for a week" (or for a certain number of days). This invitation is really a negotiated deal: If students still don't want to do the activities of the lesson after a week of participation, I have to come up with something else for them to do. Fortunately, despite having many students who often feel defeated or alienated by their experiences in schools (including PE), I have had only a few students who take me up on my deal. When they do, we make a verbal contract—for example, a fitness routine that includes stretching, sit-ups, push-ups, and run-walking.

Level III: Struggles With Empowerment

At each step in the empowerment progression, some students seem to have trouble. In the preceding fitness example, some have trouble doing the fitness routine they have learned, and I need to take them through it again. Others can do the posted routine on their own but then get stuck. Still others race ahead, developing and putting into practice a full-scale fitness program. In one of my programs, students progressed from less than 2 minutes to 15 minutes of Level III time without any problems, in martial arts no less!

Strategies for Facilitating Empowerment

Sometimes counseling time helps kids get unstuck. If a few individual students have trouble creating or carrying out a personal plan, you can give them more structure. Sometimes it just takes a slight adjustment or push. I had one student who needed me to tell him what he was supposed to do even though he had a step-by-step plan written out! (I just went down the list and said, "Do this, then do this . . .") He faced many problems at home and in school, and this modification met his needs better. If the entire group is struggling, you can address the issue in a group meeting (maybe they don't understand what is expected).

Students sometimes try to get out of doing the plan they chose or devised. When they whine about their plan, I might say, "Sure, change it and write up your change," while gently and then more forcefully reminding them that the point is to stick with something so that they can progress toward their goals. Sometimes they want to achieve the goal—for example, to lose weight—but they want to do what their friends are doing or what they perceive to be fun at the moment. "Change the goal," I say. "Can I do both losing weight and have fun?" one student asked. "Make the plan," I said. She did. Her plan was to run and then do what her friends were doing. Weeks later she asked, "Do I have to do this running in my plan?" "No," I replied. "Write down the changes in your goal and your plan." "I think I'll run instead!" she said, and off she went.

Students don't necessarily choose activities that are weaknesses. Choosing to work on one's strengths is acceptable; in fact, developing one's uniqueness in the form of a specialization is part of the definition of Level III. But it is also important to address weaknesses and problems, especially those issues that affect one's self-image. To "be like Mike" (Michael Jordan) requires dribbling and shooting with the nondominant hand, yet few students choose to practice an activity that would make them appear awkward or unskilled. You should therefore pick out some of the more common weaknesses in a group and raise the question with them during awareness talks, group meetings, or counseling time.

The accordion principle can be used to adjust the amount of Level III time in relation to the responsibility of individual students or the group. You can reduce the time on those days when students have difficulty staying on task and lengthen it on days when students are diligent in carrying out their plans. Although sometimes it may be appropriate to cut back the group's Level III time, you should never use reduced Level III time as punishment. A reduction in Level III time should be a logical consequence of their not yet being ready to take on this magnitude of personal responsibility or not being motivated to be at that stage. In this case, be certain that you do not penalize responsible students for the irresponsibility of others.

Courage to Resist Peer Pressure

The essence of Levels II and III is self-development (just as the essence of Levels I and IV is human decency). Self-development requires that students engage in sufficient self-reflection to set goals that reflect their unique needs and interests and, as they get older, their possible futures (McLaughlin and Heath 1993). But self-reflection, as difficult as that is for some of us, pales in comparison to carrying out one's goals in the face of what's cool or in with other kids. Subcultural and cultural influences are hard to sidestep, not the least of which in our electronic age is advertising.

I know of no way to place a moratorium on cultural and peer pressure. In physical education in particular, what kids do is visible to others and therefore more open to criticism. Creating a TPSR climate in your gym does help. For example, invoking the self-control rule of Level I helps ("learn to control your mouth!"), and so does talking about peer pressure. Bring it up directly and challenge your students to rise above it. Use examples from class if you can do it without putting someone on the spot (unless he or she really deserves it and might benefit by the feedback in public).

One time I gave fifth graders in a track-and-field unit three choices: a competitive track meet, a personal-best track meet, and jogging. Before they chose, I simply said, "If the way you choose is to go with your friends, that's fine with me as long as you understand that you're not making your own choice." You could hear a pin drop as they went off to their choices! Sometimes a reminder is all it takes.

Level IV: Helping and Leadership Problems

Helping others can be carried out with less than honorable intentions. For one thing, it can be characterized by arrogance. Some students, feeling superior, will "wipe their help" on others, whether they want the help or not. For another, students may view helping as a way to please the teacher or earn an extrinsic reward. That's why Level IV stresses caring, compassion, sensitivity, and responsiveness. Caring and compassion come from inside oneself; they are different motives for helping than receiving some external reward or operating from feelings of superiority. Only someone who is sensitive to a classmate's needs and wants can then be responsive to those needs. Such student leaders would not "wipe their help" on anyone.

You should build these things into any lesson that includes helping or leadership roles, but unless you really know your kids and are extremely careful in selecting helpers and leaders, problems will arise. This is especially true for students who have demonstrated leadership abilities but as time passes begin to slack off. The accordion principle applies, but reducing a student's responsibility in the

KidQuotes

"I know I did wrong things but he stayed with me."—Eighth grader

"When someone messes up I don't get mad now. I just tell them they can do better."—Eighth grader

"I learned more about coinciding with people that aren't so easy to get along with than in another class ever."—High school freshman

middle of the lesson could exacerbate the problem. Sometimes standing behind the helper or leader and quietly giving him or her one-sentence feedback—for example, saying, "Be more positive"—can correct the problem. Sometimes you'll have to call the student aside for some quick counseling time. Letting these issues slide is easy, but helpers and leaders who abuse their responsibility can harm other students. By role modeling inappropriate Level IV attitudes and behaviors, they also impede your efforts to teach TPSR.

You may believe, as some do, that behavior precedes beliefs, that a student can at first practice being a helper or leader for the wrong reasons as long as helping takes place. My only concern is that the true meaning of Level IV might be lost unless you continue to emphasize the importance of caring, sensitivity, and responsiveness. At the very least, keep a watchful eye out for abuses.

Level V: Specific Problems Outside the Gym

Level V problems do not interrupt the smooth implementation of TPSR nearly as much as problems at the other levels. However, Level V problems can intrude. For example:

- One of your students is suspended for involvement in outside-the-gym activities, such as a fight.
- A teacher complains to you about one of your student's classroom (or playground) behavior.
- One of your student's parents tells you that the student is not taking more responsibility at home (for example, taking out the garbage without being asked).

In all of these examples, one-on-one counseling time might help the student talk about the issue, tell his or her side, and perhaps set specific goals. These incidents can also be brought up in the awareness talk or group meeting (without names, of course) to remind all the kids of their Level V responsibility. I meet with my students' classroom teachers as a group every semester to get feedback on their classroom progress. My students know about these meetings, and I report back in general what their teachers say about being responsible. (Of course, taking responsibility in teachers' classrooms whose respect for students' rights and feelings is not prioritized is asking a lot, but students need to learn that they never win in confrontations with their teacher.)

Take-Aways

Here are some things from this chapter that you might consider taking with you:

- Self-reflection and self-assessment are of paramount importance in fattening your bag of tricks for addressing problems and situations that crop up in class.

- Reflection-in-action augments self-reflection by cultivating the ability to react on your feet to new and unexpected problems in class. Making solution banks is one practical way to improve your reflection-in-action.

- Level I problems and situations include a variety of discipline issues as well as conflict resolution. To address these problems successfully, a continuum of strategies is available, from negotiation with the involved student or students to the implementation of behavior modification as a last resort.

- Teaching by invitation can sometimes solve Level II problems.

- At Level III, strategies are available to help students who struggle with the independence you give them or with having the courage to make their own decisions rather than succumb to peer pressure.

- Helping others and leadership roles require specific skills as well as compassion for, and sensitivity and responsiveness to, others. When students don't possess these skills and affective qualities, problems can arise. Your awareness of what is required facilitates the development of Level IV.

- Even Level V issues sometimes need to be addressed in class.

Chapter 7

TEACHER-STUDENT RELATIONSHIP

To a great extent teachers are the curriculum: affect, attitude, and persona have a much more powerful impact on classes than do [the subject matter] or the pedagogical techniques they employ. —Rosetta Marantz Cohen

Of the four TPSR themes described in chapter 2, the teacher-student relationship is the most important. Without a certain kind of relationship, nothing else—not integrating personal and social responsibility into physical education, not empowerment, not transfer to the wider world—will work very well. "Show me a good curriculum and a mediocre teacher," I've often said, "and I'll show you a mediocre program." This is especially true for TPSR.

FOUR RELATIONAL QUALITIES

The teacher-student relationship is a series of interactions among human beings characterized by feelings, subjective perceptions, and a whole host of factors; in short, it is a complex human process, difficult to grasp let alone do effectively, full of soft truths that are difficult to measure. Some interpret this relationship as a mixture of artistry and charisma, whereas others argue that it requires specific pedagogical skills. In an effort to highlight the most important aspects of the kind of teacher-student relationship needed for TPSR, chapter 2 described four student qualities that the teacher must recognize and respect. They are repeated here in abbreviated form:

- Each student has strengths, not just deficiencies that need to be fixed. By recognizing and building on strengths, students are more likely to be open to working on their issues, such as getting angry when things don't go their way.

• Each is an individual and wants to be recognized as such, despite the uniformity of attire, slang, gestures, and so on. Gender matters, of course, and so does race and ethnicity, but students want to be recognized and respected for who they are individually as well as collectively, for their strengths and potentials. In short, "teach individuals, not classes" (Dill 1998, 66).

• Each knows things the teacher does not; each has a voice, an opinion, a side that needs to be heard.

• Each has the capacity, if not the experience, to make good decisions; often, they just need practice, as they do in learning a motor skill. If given the opportunity, they will make mistakes, but that's an important part of the process. Self-reflection needs to accompany decision making to help students become more reflective about the choices they make.

Working from kids' strengths shifts the focus from how incomplete and inadequate they are to a positive base from which to work. Recognizing and respecting their individuality conveys to them that everyone starts in a different place and has unique strengths, capacities, needs, and interests. Giving students a voice in the process and turning some choices and decisions over to them are central to promoting empowerment and responsibility. All of these relational qualities lay the foundation for TPSR by treating kids with dignity, modeling human decency, and promoting self-development.

Noddings (1992) argued that "formulaic approaches [to caring are] hopeless," that caring is an "ethic of relation." Although there is justification for warning against formulaic approaches, it is necessary somehow to comprehend the "ethic of relation." Temporarily reducing the complexity of the teacher-student relationship to recognizing and respecting the preceding four qualities has several benefits:

• You can understand and respect those student qualities, a truth that contradicts claims like "teachers are born not made" or "you gotta have charisma."

• Treating kids these ways creates a respectful climate in your gym. Once you establish that, instituting the levels and the TPSR lesson-plan format and instructional strategies becomes much easier.

• Your students will begin to treat you the same way! But they won't necessarily treat their peers this way; that's why you need Level I.

• Although honoring these four qualities in students does not mean you have mastered the kind of teacher-student relationship needed for TPSR, it does get your foot in the door and open opportunities to develop other qualities and skills that will enhance this relationship.

BLEEDING-HEART LIBERALS NEED NOT APPLY

None of this means being a "touchy feely" bleeding-heart liberal or some kind of rescuer driven by a messiah complex, however well intentioned! As Walt Schafer (1992, 488), quoting T.J. Hurley, wrote:

> Being tender-hearted does not mean being soft-hearted. . . . Creative altruists work in the most challenging situations. Those they serve—youth at risk, addicts and drug abusers, juvenile delinquents, the mentally ill, the homeless—are unimpressed by do-gooders and bleeding-heart liberals. But their lives are transformed by the pragmatic intelligence and unconditional support they encounter in creative altruists.

Hal Adams, who works with adults in Chicago inner-city communities, added that respect for those with whom one works is essential, that you can't come in with the attitude that "you've got problems and I'm here to fix them" (thanks to Hal for this example).

RELATIONAL QUALITIES AND COUNSELING TIME

Counseling time (described more fully in chapter 4) is a specific time set aside to connect one on one with your students. I have found counseling time particularly valuable because there are many barriers between me and my students, and each one makes our relationship harder. Differences in age (I keep getting older yet they stay the same age), gender, education, socioeconomic status, race, and ethnicity combine to form a high wall between us. I try to poke little holes in that wall by talking to each student individually for a few seconds as often as I can during a designated counseling time or whenever I have the opportunity. I just tell them that it's nice to have them here today or ask how they are doing or if everything is OK. I mention something particular to them if I can, such as "Been practicing your jump shot?" or "That's a good-looking shirt." In all cases my intention is to welcome them, to treat them as worthy of personal attention, and to show that I care about them as individuals.

Of course, this strategy only works if I do in fact care, do perceive each student as worthwhile, and am sensitive enough to say something that dignifies him or her. Students don't always respond, and sometimes they look away. But so far no one has ever outright rejected one of my personal welcomes or walked away while I was talking. A bit of courage is necessary to keep offering this gesture if a student isn't responsive. You should seek feedback to be certain that kids perceive your efforts in the way you intend. Specific strategies such as group meetings, reflection time, and anonymous program evaluations provide opportunities to calibrate perceptions.

TEACHER QUALITIES AND SKILLS

Honoring the four relational qualities is foundational to TPSR, but these four qualities do not fully characterize the complexities of the teacher-student relationship. Let's explore this complexity a bit further.

The Person of the Teacher

The curriculum we put into practice as teachers, whether TPSR-based or not, is certainly important and often difficult, but it won't matter much if the instructor-student relationship is flawed. In this era of subject-matter standards and accountability, we need to be reminded of the importance of who the teacher is. As Bill Ayers (1989, 130) wrote:

> [T]here is no clear line delineating the person and the teacher. Rather, there is a seamless web between teaching and being, between teacher and person. Teaching is not simply what one does, it is who one is.

A sign seen at a teacher's conference reaffirms this notion: "We teach who we are" (Lickona 1991, 71). David Denton (1972, 74) states a similar idea: "Teaching is you, as you embody history, embody mathematics. . . . The question is not *what* to teach. The question is not *how* to teach. The question is *who* is teaching?"

Are Ayers, Lickona, and Denton right? Partly, I think. What and how we teach matters too, but as Nel Noddings (1992, 8) wrote, "Educational research . . . has made the error of supposing that method can be substituted for individuals." Larry Cuban (1993, 184) said that curriculum reformers always get it wrong, because they do not understand that "at the heart of [instruction] is the personal relationship between [teacher] and students that develops over matters of content."

What kind of a person should the TPSR teacher be? The simple answer is that the teacher needs to live the levels and themes, to "embody" TPSR, to use Denton's term. This embodiment has a number of dimensions, most of which support or reinforce the four relational qualities mentioned earlier.

Sense of Purpose

Some teachers I've known seem to go through the motions without much apparent passion. They may have lost the fire, but my years of involvement with preservice teachers suggest that intrinsic interest in teaching kids varies with them as well. I call this passion "sense of purpose." If you have it, it's your answer to "What's worth doing," to "What kind of contribution do I want to make?" It's the essence of your motivation, the source of your passion. To possess this sense of purpose in teaching, caring about and connecting with kids must bring "fulfillment through satisfaction, through the knowledge that one has been true to her/his value of enhancing others, whether or not others express their appreciation or indebtedness" (Schafer 1992, 488).

Embodying TPSR means that the levels and themes need to be central to your sense of purpose, to the quality and strength of your vision about making a contribution to kids' lives. TPSR becomes the "moral intention to develop a certain kind of human being" (Goodlad 1988, 109), what you believe in and cherish (Greene 1986). Only those teachers who believe in and cherish personal and social responsibility as the moral vision for kids can truly embody it.

Listening and Caring

But sense of purpose is not enough. One also needs to be able to respect students as unique individuals who have their own values, perceptions, fears, and aspirations and who deserve to be acknowledged, listened to, negotiated with—in short, to be cared about and treated with dignity. Gordon (1999, 305) put it this way: "Effective . . . teachers want to be partners with their students."

Listening is an important way to care and to treat kids with dignity. When we listen, they feel as if they count, and we learn some things (which is especially important when our backgrounds are different). One of the things we can learn is what John Nicholls (Nicholls and Hazzard 1993) calls the kids' theories of curriculum—for example, that physical education ought to be for playing—which often conflict with the teacher's theories (such as TPSR). Listening is also a necessary skill for engaging in individual decision making and group-meeting strategies.

In one inner-city junior high, at-risk students said that the teachers who helped them were those that noticed them and asked about them, listened to them, respected them, and gave them chances (Schlosser 1992). Quincy Howe (1991, 84, 86), who works with inner-city special-education adolescents in a residential setting, put it this way: "A child must be convinced that the adult can be counted on to act in his best interest. This turns out to be an enormous and daunting piece of work. . . . At issue are his doubts, both as to whether he can do the job and whether I will continue to believe in his abilities." Ennis and colleagues (1999, 167) conducted extensive interviews with "disruptive and disengaged students" in PE and concluded that they "are unwilling to learn when teachers remain aloof . . . and refuse to spend time with students or express interest in their lives."

Bill Rose says to his secondary school students, "If at any time in class you feel you're being abused by me, or I'm embarrassing you in front of the whole class, you have to let me know. I don't know how everybody feels" (Lickona 1991, 73). Rose's admission that he doesn't know everything, that he needs some help, encourages his students to share their thoughts with him. It also shows his desire to listen to them, to try to understand their side of things. He wants to know how his students are feeling, but they need to help him do so. When my students do or say something I don't understand, I am often afraid to ask for fear of being perceived as out of it or uncool. Yet when I do, I usually learn something and am probably a more sensitive teacher as a result. The kids don't seem to mind.

Genuineness and Vulnerability

Caring about kids requires more than talking and listening. It also requires being genuine with them. Being genuine does not involve trying to copy their dress and gestures and talk their language, unless, of course, one is part of their subculture. Being genuine does not mean being nasty if one is in a bad mood or sharing details about one's last love affair. To me it means being oneself (to a point) rather than trying to be cool. It means owning one's beliefs rather than turning them into generic mandates for everyone. It also means expressing one's humanity in appropriate ways. I am not always right. I don't live in the gym; I have another life. I am not always upbeat. Most of all, being genuine means caring sincerely about students and believing in their essential dignity and worth. Otherwise, talking and listening to kids won't have validity.

Genuineness also means being vulnerable. Telling kids, "I blew it," whether referring to a volleyball serve or an attempt to solve some problem, points out my recognition that I don't get everything right every time. Students who are potential discipline problems may see vulnerability as a weakness that they can exploit. Yet when dealing with someone who is out of control and being disruptive or abusive, I have found that saying, "Am I the problem?" calms things down and gets us into the issues (which may be me but often is not).

This strategy works well in a one-to-one meeting, where there is no audience to play to. But you can ask the same question, "Am I the problem?" and reveal the same vulnerability, in group meetings when the group has had a bad day or something has gone wrong. After one lesson in which the kids were off task and argumentative with each other, I asked what I was doing wrong. "You need to be tougher on us," one boy said. Another added, "Make us do push-ups when we're bad." So we talked about my style, the purpose of the program (getting tough on yourself is your job in TPSR), and how we might compromise.

Of course, you have to be ready for the constant scrutiny of students once they become aware of the genuineness factor. During a fitness session, one kid yelled to me: "You ain't doin' the exercises!" My response? I dropped down and started doing push-ups!

Vulnerability, like other things, makes sense to a point. Martin Buber told Carl Rogers that Rogers was wrong about the teacher-student relationship being equal. According to Buber, it is unequal by its very nature. The student comes to the teacher for help. "You are able, more or less, to help him. . . . you see him. . . . he cannot, by far, see you" (in Noddings 1992, 107). To balance vulnerability, the teacher must be able to confront students, to call them on their abusiveness, their argumentativeness, their lack of effort, their lack of other-directedness, their egocentrism, and so on. "What they really need is a teacher who will face them, seek eye contact, deflect their jibes and evasions, and tell them what they need to know" (Howe 1991, 66). You cannot substitute vulnerability and confrontation for each other. You need both.

Intuition and Self-Reflection

Another piece of the teacher-student interaction puzzle is intuition, which Rubin (1985) has described as recognizing and acting on clues. Intuition seems to me to be a fancy word for sizing up my class when they come in the door. What is their collective mood? What individual issues are noticeable? For every lesson, no matter what I've planned, I need to ask the question, What can I get away with? That is, how much personal and social responsibility can I put across to this group in this lesson? How much can I push or challenge my students? What will they put up with before rebelling or shutting down? Although this approach emerged from years of work with at-risk kids, I find it useful in my university classes as well. I try to sense the receptivity of the group, the rhythm of the lesson. Then I apply the accordion principle, giving more or less responsibility, longer or shorter awareness talks, and so on.

Intuition needs to be reinforced with perseverance. I need to outlast the kids! By that I mean students (and other stakeholders) may resist the notion of a program based on personal and social responsibility. Self-direction? Caring? (How uncool!) A choice of whether to compete or improve? No referees? Talking and writing? Counseling time? New ideas, although sometimes attractive, are almost never easy to implement, especially with older kids. To be successful, you must resolve that you won't give up or back off putting your sense of purpose and your ideas into practice. One of my ninth-grade students, a reasonably skilled performer who was used to being able to play the whole PE period, wrote an essay about my class for his English class titled "PE Makes You Hate." Ouch! Teaching anything new is provocative. You must have inner strength to pull it off.

Being able to size up individuals and groups to determine how much they can handle and sticking with your ideas are essential qualities. Sizing up is part of the larger habit of self-reflection, discussed in the last chapter in relation to problems that arise in class. Sizing up yourself by self-reflection is also part of TPSR; in fact, it is fundamental. What is your mood? What are your issues in this class? Moreover, how can you exhort students to be more reflective if you are unreflective? How can you exhort students to become more responsible without being responsible yourself, without being as reflective as possible about embodying personal and social responsibility? How strong is your self-motivation (Level II)? Your self-direction (Level III)? Your sensitivity and responsiveness to students' rights, feelings, and needs (Levels I and IV)?

Cultivating the habit of professional self-reflection by keeping a daily journal, by being open to criticism, by making and evaluating

KidQuotes

"You're proof that white men can't jump!"—Sixth grader to Don

"You ain't doin' the exercises!"—High school junior to Don

"In your class you could always learn something . . . about how to deal and cope with everyday life and reality. Although your class was PE, I learned a great deal more . . . made me take pride in myself . . . and not be quick to judge other people. (PS If you can find time between push-ups and sit-ups, drop me a letter)."—Letter from former high school student

"I learned that it doesn't pay to put on an image of being tough. . . . When you feel down and out and read this letter, it better warm you up or I might have to fly to Chicago to beat some sense into you."—Letter from former high school student

personal change is perhaps the single most effective method for improving all these qualities.

I like to talk to teachers about their chaos threshold, by which I mean how much chaos they can tolerate in a lesson. Some need to tiptoe into the empowerment strategies. Student freedom makes them nervous. I say, "No problem. Don't exceed your chaos threshold, but try to push it a bit." Reflection helps us to recognize such problems, to think about solutions, and to evaluate these solutions in practice.

Georgiadis' (1990) struggles to reconcile the values he learned as a professional basketball player with the values that underlie TPSR provide an excellent example of the often painful process of self-reflection. In his first experience with at-risk youth in an after-school basketball program, he found himself screaming at the referees (who were volunteering their time), playing only the most talented kids, and making all the decisions. His students rebelled, and he found himself sunk in a deeply personal struggle of conflicting values. He found that to make TPSR work, he needed to shift some decisions to the students and listen to their input. These strategies conflicted with the professional sport model, so it was an agonizing process that took persistent self-reflection to resolve.

Sense of Humor and Playful Spirit

Attempting to be a caring, genuine, empathetic, intuitive teacher has its price. When I watched Robin Williams as a teacher in *Dead Poets Society,* I thought, "Oh, to be able to teach like that." But could a Robin Williams do that period after period and day after day? Howe (1991, 67) said no: "The trouble is that such [teaching] performances are enormously draining and I am good for only one or two a day." He found after four years of teaching in a residential home that his willingness to share his breaks with students was "not what it used to be" (p. 143).

A sense of humor and a playful spirit are effective guards against burnout. Keeping kids focused on responsibility is hard work, and you need to compensate for it by using a light touch, at least from time to time. The essence of a sense of humor is an attitude that sees the humor in everyday life without, as kids often do, needing someone to bear the brunt of the joke. The most important aspect of humor is to be able to laugh at oneself. Howe (1991, 27) often turned a serious situation into something humorously self-critical. For example, to a student who exclaimed that she was bored, he said, "I once had a student die of boredom in my class." A playful spirit involves many things, including being upbeat and enthusiastic (but only genuinely so), having fun with the kids, and celebrating with high fives or low fives or whatever the latest fad is.

Teaching Students With Different Cultural Backgrounds

I am a white male. I have taught in urban multicultural settings, and I now teach in urban settings where all students and most teachers and administrators are African American, Mexican American, or Mexican immigrant. These settings sorely test my embodiment of TPSR, and the barriers of race, ethnicity, education, and socioeconomic status are particularly difficult to negotiate. I have found, by trial and error, a few guidelines that seem to help in this process. Some of them might help if your students have different backgrounds from yours (including difference in gender).

Don't Try To Be Cool

Being oneself, being genuine, is crucial. Kids quickly spot a phony. I have found it best not to worry about doing fancy handshakes or using street language. Some of these things evolve with time, but they aren't important. The teacher's sincere concern for the kids and respect for them and their culture are far more important. Howe (1991) was the only staff member to wear a coat and tie in a school for at-risk kids, rendering him a high-profile target for student humor. He persisted—it was him—and the humorous jabs disappeared with time.

Not trying to be popular is difficult. The fear of not being liked is always lurking in the back of my mind, but I try not to let it control me. The best antidote I've found is successful experiences with kids when I am myself.

Learn About and Respect the Culture

Being oneself has limits. Having at least general knowledge of the culture with which you are working is helpful. Delpit's (1988, 93) example of the difference between a caring white parent who says to her child, "Isn't it time for your bath?" and the caring African-American parent who says, "Boy, get your rusty behind in that bathtub!" is an example of this point. Being prepared for and being able to accept cultural differences is essential in becoming an effective teacher of students whose backgrounds differ from yours.

Teachers must be wary of cultural preconceptions, even those that seem sympathetic. For example, research suggests that self-concept among African-American youth is not lower than that of white youth, though their perception of empowerment may be (Murray, Smith, and West 1989). As another example, many whites would be surprised to learn that the traditional American work ethic enjoys substantial support among African Americans. Bredemeier's (1988) study of urban minority teachers shows that although they recognize existing social problems, they have not wavered from teaching hard work, perseverance, self-responsibility, and orientation to the future. In addition, though it is regrettable, the criminal sector often does a better job of harnessing the energy of inner-city youth than mainstream society does, such as in drug trafficking.

On the other hand, teachers must be prepared to understand behaviors that do not reflect white middle-class norms. Foster (1974) described some of these characteristics among inner-city high school students: style and flare as part of the student's performance, physical aggression and impregnating a female as signs of manhood, and such skills as manipulating, taunting, and verbal assault as requirements for street survival. Howe's (1991, 32) description of the difference between his low-income male and female students is another example. The male model is the "rigid jaw and unmoist eye . . . [and a] playful and evasive way of dealing with experience" whereas females are "more tempestuous, more ungoverned" and tend to "make full disclosure of the intensity of their feelings."

Respect Your Students

Respect for the culture and especially for the kids is a key to accepting differences. Recognize their strengths and individual selves, and give them opportunities to express their views and make decisions. The approach I have found most useful is to listen to my students. I begin to learn their theories and perceptions of life, school, and physical activity and something of their culture. Group meetings and counseling time can help here, but the openness of teachers to ideas and perceptions different from their own is fundamental to making these strategies work.

I sometimes need to remind myself that the in-the-moment mentality of adolescents allows them to see the humor and pathos of the moment, whereas my focus on what's ahead prevents me from sharing their observations and insights. Other times I laugh in spite of myself.

Take-Aways

Here are some things from this chapter that you might consider taking with you:

- Recognizing and respecting your students' strengths, individuality, voices, and capacity for decision making reduces the complexity of the teacher-student relationship and creates a climate in which TPSR can grow.

- A set-aside counseling time facilitates brief one-on-one meetings to express your recognition of and respect for those four qualities in your students.
- Of the specific skills and qualities that further facilitate the teacher-student relationship, perhaps the most important is having a sense of purpose, but other qualities are important as well, among them listening and caring, genuineness and vulnerability, intuition (sizing things up from clues), self-reflections, and a sense of humor.
- Teaching students with different cultural backgrounds takes the same skills and qualities, especially recognizing and respecting the four student qualities. You must be yourself while at the same time knowing what you don't know, being open to unfamiliar values and customs, and learning as much as you can about cultures other than your own that are represented among your students.

Chapter 8

ASSESSMENT

Those personal qualities that we hold dear are exceedingly difficult to assess, [so] we are apt to measure what we can, and eventually come to value what is measured. —Arthur Wise

Schools typically evaluate students, teachers, and the curriculum in practice (or functional curriculum). Of these, student assessment receives the highest priority, although the standards-accountability movement has influenced teacher evaluation and curricular decision making as well. For TPSR to work effectively, all three kinds of evaluation need to be approached in certain ways. Self-assessment—described in chapter 6 as a process of discovery involving reflection and discussion, followed by information-based action, and leading to an ongoing process of strengthening what works or is promising (Camino 2002, 40)—is central in all three kinds of evaluation.

Student Evaluation

Student evaluation ought to reflect the presence of TPSR in two ways: first, by giving students feedback on your perceptions of the extent to which they are taking personal and social responsibility in class, and second, by empowering students to share in the evaluation process.

Feedback in Group Meeting and Reflection Time

Both of these approaches are built into the group meeting and reflection time parts of the lesson-plan format. The group meeting enables students to evaluate the class as a whole and comment about how specific individuals acted in class that day, when they learn to do so respectfully and as positively as they can. Sometimes in the group meeting, students will criticize other students—for example, for not cooperating or losing their temper. You must handle this carefully, but as long as the student or students being criticized have an opportunity to respond and the process is carried out respectfully, both you and the involved students receive feedback. You also have an opportunity to share your feedback with students, not only about the process but also about whether the criticism was justified. In addition, you should encourage student leaders or coaches to tell everyone how their assignment—their minilesson or the team they coached—went and what positive contributions the students they worked with made to the group or team. Again, this approach provides feedback for the named students as well as you (along with the benefit of pointing out student role models of Level IV), and it gives you an opportunity to share your feedback.

You must, however, share your feedback last! You are only one voice in this process, but you will usurp the students' authority to share their views if you talk first. Of course, you can take over—this isn't a full-fledged democracy, although it should be heading in that direction. But you should take control only when necessary. Sometimes kids need guidance, for example, on how to talk to each other or how to focus or listen more, but too much "guidance" can set back the empowerment process. Just monitor yourself and the class so that you achieve a balance and kids' voices are respected.

Reflection time more directly addresses student evaluation, because the point is to have students evaluate themselves on how well they put the levels into practice that day. If they point their thumbs, raise their hands, hold up a number of fingers, or tap in and out, you receive feedback of their perceptions and can make occasional comments—"Yes, I saw that," "You're being hard on yourself," "I thought that needed some work," "Should that be a goal for you?" If you use journals or workbooks, even occasionally, you can give written feedback.

Rubrics

The rubric shown in form 8.1, although "excessively general" for a rubric according to one assessment expert, at least illustrates the concept of rubric use with the levels. You can use this rubric, appropriately tightened and worded to be age appropriate, to give your students feedback or to grade their personal and social responsibility.

If you have student leaders, you might be able to have them use the rubric to evaluate students they have worked with. You can also ask your students to evaluate themselves using the rubric. These three different uses of the rubric can comprise a progression from teacher directed to student directed, or both you and your students can fill out rubrics and compare notes.

Another way to share power with students is to ask for their input into the development of a responsibility rubric. Who knows? They might come up with one that is not excessively general!

Form 8.1

Responsibility Rubric

	Consistently	Sporadically	Seldom	Never
Contributes to own well-being:				
Effort and self-motivation	___	___	___	___
Independence	___	___	___	___
Goal setting	___	___	___	___
Contributes to others' well-being:				
Respect	___	___	___	___
Helping	___	___	___	___
Leadership	___	___	___	___

From Teaching Responsibility Through Physical Education,
Second Edition *by Don Hellison, 2003, Champaign, IL: Human Kinetics.*

Hichwa (1998) had his middle school PE students grade themselves with a modified rubric: done consistently, done most of the time, or done inconsistently. They wrote their self-grades on a five-by-seven-inch card for

- works to personal best,
- follows rules and is cooperative,
- takes care of equipment,
- is thoughtful and helpful to others, and
- improves fitness and skill scores.

He also graded each student in the same way and met individually with students whose ratings did not match his to discuss the differences. In addition, he used an attendance form to record his observations that day, using

- 1 for works and tries hard,
- 2 for follows rules,
- 3 for respects equipment,
- 4 for respects others, and
- 5 for cares for and helps others.

If the behavior was negative, he placed a minus next to the number. This system gave him specific data to discuss with his kids.

I created a self-evaluation approach for skill development based on rubrics. From time to time, I hand students a list of the skills we are learning and practicing and ask them to rate themselves. (This could also be done orally.) The evaluation categories range from a low score of 1 to a high score of 5:

- 1 = I haven't tried it yet.
- 2 = I'm working on it.
- 3 = I can demonstrate it correctly.
- 4 = I can perform it correctly in a game or situation.
- 5 = I can teach it to someone so that they learn it correctly.

For this to work, you will probably have to take some time to teach your students what each category means. I have used this system with both middle and high school students, and most of them needed help to get started. They did, however, express interest in evaluating their skills this way after they understood what to do. These numbers can be converted to grades, giving students an opportunity to grade themselves on individual skills. In such a conversion, 5 would convert to A, reinforcing the importance of Level IV.

Concerning student evaluation, the rubric examples give students the opportunity to measure themselves in comparison to some set categories. Workbooks provide another opportunity for students to evaluate themselves on the levels and their development in fitness, motor skills, and conceptual knowledge. Our students, most of whom are not particularly fond of writing, love charting their progress in their workbooks!

Jerry Guthrie's workbook *Be Your Own Coach* (1982) used soccer to illustrate some creative ways for students to measure their own progress. They are shown in form 8.2 and figure 8.1.

Self-Grading

In the above rubric examples, one option is for teachers to use rubrics to grade their students. This practice, however, has serious limitations:

> As long as grading is not part of the assessment process, the feedback from assessment can facilitate the development of responsibility. However . . . if a teacher links assessment to grading, students must share in this process in order to be true to [TPSR]. . . . Truly authentic assessment [of responsibility] must . . . include a gradual shift in responsibility from the teacher to the students (Parker and Hellison 2001, 27).

Form 8.2

Measuring Your Skills

You can measure soccer skills and body fitness in several ways:

1. Counting: How many juggles?
2. Timing: How fast through cones?
3. Accuracy: How many accurate shots?

Sometimes you may combine two or more of these measurements:

How many hops over the ball in 30 seconds?

Adapted, by permission, from D. Hellison, 1985, Goals and strategies for teaching physical education, *(Champaign, IL: Human Kinetics), 79.*

From Teaching Responsibility Through Physical Education,
Second Edition *by Don Hellison, 2003, Champaign, IL: Human Kinetics.*

Keeping regular and accurate records of your self-coached practice is easy when you follow a few simple ideas:

1. *Keep your recording simple and convenient.* Carrying a three-by-five index card or notebook will allow you to make regular recordlng of your skill measurements.

2. *Transfer your measurements from the small record to a permanent chart.* A wall chart posted in a conspicuous place will allow you to see how your measurements look over a long period.

Figure 8.1   Record-keeping tips.

Adapted, by permission, from D. Hellison, 1985, Goals and strategies for teaching physical education, *(Champaign, IL: Human Kinetics), 81.*

Self-grading can be done in other ways as well. Lambert and Grube (1988) had their high school students in Rock Springs, Wyoming, grade themselves using the responsibility levels. The teachers scheduled conferences to resolve conflicts between their grades and those of their students. The result became part of the grade. Junior high school teacher Jeff Walsh and high school teachers Gayle McDonald and Tom Hinton created the self-grading scorecard shown in form 8.3 to offer students input on their grade. They developed one-sentence descriptors for various aspects of each level, perhaps

Form 8.3

Self-Grading Scorecard

Level	Behavior	Self-grade	Teacher grade
I	Does not call others names	____	____
I	Controls temper	____	____
I	Does not disrupt class	____	____
II	On time to class	____	____
II	Tries new activities	____	____
II	Listens to instructions	____	____
III	Makes and follows contract	____	____
III	Writes in journal every day	____	____
IV	Shares equipment	____	____
IV	Treats others kindly	____	____
IV	Shows good sportsmanship	____	____

Adapted, by permission, from D. Hellison, 1985, Goals and strategies for teaching physical education *(Champaign, IL: Human Kinetics), 21.*

From Teaching Responsibility Through Physical Education,
Second Edition by Don Hellison, 2003, Champaign, IL: Human Kinetics.

so no one could accuse them of being excessively general! Both students and the teacher grade students on each component, and the teacher then assigns a grade by considering student input.

Because I had not yet conceived of Level V when Jeff, Gayle, and Tom created their scorecard, they could not have included it without an extremely creative effort. Even now, exclusion of Level V is a common practice of in-school physical education teachers, as I pointed out in an earlier chapter. Although I usually view such omissions as a flaw in the practice of TPSR, grading is about student performance (et cetera) in your class, so Level V is irrelevant. Classroom teachers often grade affective and social factors, especially pre-high school, so if your students are graded for these things on their report cards you could check on some of their responsibilities outside the gym. For example, my fourth-grade through eighth-grade students are graded on self-control, so I can look for improvements on their report cards and by talking with their classroom teachers.

Redefining Success in Self-Grading

Chapter 5 includes a set of Level II strategies to help your students redefine success so that, with sufficient effort, they can reach it. If you use norms or standards for grading as promoted by the standards-accountability movement, redefining success is not an option. Because that movement tends to marginalize physical education in schools, though, it does permit individual PE teachers more freedom to develop a grading system that makes philosophical sense to them. One approach that makes TPSR sense is to build redefining success into your grading system. Rubrics don't do that, and neither does the self-grading scorecard.

Building redefining success into your grading system pretty much eliminates students' comparing grades, at least in relation to "who's best." At the same time, students must learn to respect definitions of success other than their own. Parents, especially those who have been successful in the traditional system, might not be overjoyed at such a prospect. On the other hand, if their goal is to send their child to Harvard but he scores low on fitness norms and therefore receives a low PE grade, they are likely to be more supportive of a more individualized approach.

Improvement is one measure of success. Students can choose to be graded by their improvement, especially if their performance in the skill or fitness component being assessed can be improved or, from a standards perspective, should be improved. Another way is to give students the choice of improvement or achievement or some combination.

Another kind of choice involves giving students options that assess different skills, talents, or intelligences, such as

- improvement or achievement in either a fitness test or a fitness concepts test;
- demonstration of correct form or a performance test for the volleyball underarm pass, set, hit, or serve (or choose two or three); or
- skill or fitness tests from the activities students have studied or practiced in class.

Self-Evaluation Forms

Self-evaluation forms such as the self-report shown in form 5.2 (chapter 5, pages 67-68) help students become aware of their own needs, thereby setting the stage for goal setting.

Gary Kuney combined several of these options in a contract he offered to his upper elementary and junior high students as shown in form 8.4. In this self-grading contract for fitness, he first asked students to rate their present fitness and their goal. Note that they could choose "I don't care." I've found that students treat all the choices more seriously when the full range is included. Moreover, if

Form 8.4

Gary Kuney's Self-Grading Contract

Name _____ Grade _____

Rate your present fitness level:

___ Pro   ___ Excellent   ___ Good   ___ OK   ___ So-so

___ Could be better   ___ I don't care

Where would you like to be?

___ Pro   ___ Excellent   ___ Good   ___ OK   ___ So-so

___ Could be better   ___ I don't care

Grouping I want to be in:

___ Noncompetitive   ___ Competitive

Each student must select four goals or one lab and two goals.

___ Goal A: Book report on fitness

___ Goal B: Pass test on fitness concepts

___ Goal C: Improve fitness

___ Goal D: Give written report on history

___ Goal E: Work with others in positive manner

___ Goal F: Give it your best shot

___ Goal G: Adhere to safety rules

___ Lab A: Aerobic development lab

___ Lab B: Strength development lab

I agree to fill this learning plan

Student _____

Witness (teacher) _____

Adapted, by permission, from D. Hellison, 2000, Youth development and physical activity *(Champaign, IL: Human Kinetics), 108.*

From Teaching Responsibility Through Physical Education,
Second Edition by Don Hellison, 2003, Champaign, IL: Human Kinetics.

KidQuotes

"I learned how to control my temper to other people inside and outside the gym."—Fourth grader

"I improved myself as a person because I don't talk back."—Seventh grader

"You did a good job today, but we were pitiful."—Seventh grader to Don

---

they truly don't care, I'd like to know. I want them to have the opportunity to express their low motivation to me (rather than behind my back); then we can address it. They also have a choice of whether to participate in some competitive events or not. Finally, they get to choose how they will be evaluated. Gary's contract is complicated: lots of choices for kids, lots of work for him. I include it here only to broaden your thinking about redefining success in self-grading, and it doesn't hurt any of us to see a teacher willing and able to pull off something like this.

PROGRAM EVALUATION

Attempting to evaluate the effectiveness of TPSR in your program is no simple task. State-level public education mandates often either ignore this kind of learning or reduce it to observable behaviors, as indicated by the Arthur Wise quotation that opened this chapter. As a result, self-assessment of your program is essential.

The first step in program evaluation is to assess to what extent TPSR is being implemented. TPSR cannot have much effect on students if it is not being implemented. Buchanan's (1996) study is a good example of that. She spent 120 pages describing her study and data and analyzing her results to conclude that the teachers had not bought into TPSR much and therefore did not implement much of it correctly! Separating the extent of TPSR implementation from its effect and assessing it first may alleviate this kind of problem.

You can check the extent of your implementation in this way. Keep a daily journal to reflect on the extent to which TPSR was put into practice that day and how well it worked. Set aside about five minutes a day to do this, or you can use your daily lesson plan for this purpose (write all over it in a different colored ink to differentiate your reflections from the original lesson plan notes). A shortcut is to give yourself a letter grade for the extent to which you implemented your version of TPSR.

This evaluation procedure captures the extent of implementation and your perceptions of its effectiveness. Some version of the following evaluation procedures will give you more information on the effectiveness of your program:

- Include in your journal or on your lesson plan your observations and feelings about this approach—whether it continues to make sense, whether this is something you want to stand for as a teacher. Try to separate these comments from whether the approach is working.

- Use reflection time and group-meeting comments as a source of student perceptions (write them down when you can).

- Keep track of relevant student behaviors, such as the amount of name calling, on-task participation, independent work, and helping. You can do this in several ways. You can describe level-related behaviors as completely as possible for one lesson early in the program and then again later in the program to help determine whether your students are improving. Another way is to keep track of behaviors on a regular or even daily basis—for example, by marking the appropriate level number next to each student's name.

- Consider using anonymous student evaluations of your class. Ask them what they learned about themselves, about relating to others, and if they've improved. You can also construct pre- and postquestionnaires. A knowledge test of the levels will show the extent to which the students understand the levels. Just asking students how respectful they are or how self-directed they are near the beginning of the year and then again near the end of the year may show how much insight students have into their own efforts and actions.

- Talk with the teachers, administrators, and playground or bus-duty supervisors who interact with your students to see whether they believe your classes are having any effect on the students.

TEACHER EVALUATION

Affective and social-moral development are not high on typical school district priorities, so your school may not evaluate the TPSR qualities you embody and facilitate. Therefore, you need to assess your own effectiveness in making TPSR work. After all, if something doesn't work, TPSR, which certainly is not foolproof, could be the problem. Or students rebel because they aren't ready or for some other reason. But it could be you. One way to check yourself is to grade your implementation of TPSR goals and teacher skills and qualities (chapter 7) on a daily basis in your journal.

The first time I tried this I learned two things about myself: first, that I couldn't honestly give myself anything better than a C+ for the whole first semester in a high school class that met daily, and second, that on many of the days I thought were good, my embodiment of TPSR was weak. (Upon analysis, it turned out that they were "good" because the kids didn't give me much trouble, but I didn't do much TPSR.) The teacher-student relationship skills and qualities described in the last chapter can guide your self-evaluation.

Another way to assess yourself is to provide honest answers to the TPSR teacher questionnaire shown in chapter 9, form 9.1 (page 124). If most of your answers are positive—"yes" or "I'm working on it" or "I want to do that"—you can have some confidence that you're on the right track. If you want to assess your readiness more specifically, check one of these categories for each statement:

- I am doing this now.
- I want to implement this soon.
- This is a long-range goal for me.
- I need to think about it some more.
- This isn't relevant for my situation.

We will return to the TPSR teacher questionnaire in the next chapter.

Take-Aways

Here are some things from this chapter that you might consider taking with you:

- Whether you are evaluating your students, your program, or yourself, self-assessment is an important part of the process in TPSR.
- You can assess students' personal and social responsibility with a rubric, by grading specific responsibility qualities, and in other ways. But obtaining input from students in group meetings and reflection time as well as having them fill out the rubric or responsibility quality grades themselves will not only empower them (if you pay some attention to their views) but also provide you with more information. Student self-assessment, like all empowerment strategies, requires a gradual progression.

- If you help students build their own definitions of success into individual criteria for their personal goals as well as their grades, they will be more likely to explore their unique strengths and weaknesses and expand their understanding of self-assessment (beyond evaluating themselves on your criteria).

- Program evaluation should begin with an investigation of how much and how well you have implemented TPSR. After that, you can evaluate the effectiveness of TPSR in your classes by keeping a journal, by keeping track of student behaviors and comments, by asking students to evaluate the program anonymously, and by requesting evaluations of students from outside observers such as administrators, teachers, and parents.

- If you want an evaluation of your performance as a teacher of TPSR, you will likely have to conduct it yourself. One way to do this is to grade yourself on a daily basis, especially in relation to implementation of TPSR goals and strategies as well as the teacher skills and qualities listed in chapter 7. Another way is to take the TPSR teacher questionnaire (see chapter 9, form 9.1).

Part III

IMPLEMENTATION

GETTING STARTED

The only person you really get to change is yourself. —Carolyn Boyles-Watson

Good teaching is hard work. If you are employed in a typical public school—rather than, for example, a charter or alternative school— you probably see lots of kids, have class sizes of about 30, and must deal with all the usual side jobs like lunchroom duty and after-school programs as well as bureaucratic school paperwork and policies. Even one good lesson a day costs you precious energy. Given these conditions, how can you be expected to help students become more personally and socially responsible? This chapter is intended to help you get started.

Is TPSR for You?

The last chapter ended by suggesting that you take the TPSR questionnaire shown in form 9.1 as part of your self-evaluation as a teacher of TPSR. Answering that questionnaire is perhaps the quickest way to determine whether you ought to embark on the TPSR implementation journey, as long as you understand that the statements describe an ideal version of TPSR, a distant vision for most of us. A new curriculum model is a headache for most teachers because it disrupts their practice. And because it is new, stress escalates as you cope with students who, like you, may not be used to doing physical education this way. Trying something different is, well, difficult. That's why you want to be as certain as you can at this point that TPSR is worth doing. (You should of course revisit this question down the road as well.)

From my work with teachers over the years, I get the sense that many teachers adopt TPSR as a management tool to deal with discipline in class. In reality, authentic implementation of TPSR often creates a conflict with teacher-directed classroom management strategies (see McCaslin and Good 1992). Although Mrugala's (2002) PE

Form 9.1

TPSR Teacher Questionnaire

1. Do you like kids, and can you relate to them?
2. Do you try to treat all kids as individuals?
3. Do you spend some time consciously focusing on students' strengths?
4. Do you listen to students and believe that they "know things?"
5. Do you share your power as a teacher with students?
6. Do you help your students to solve their own conflicts so that they can do this on their own?
7. Do you help your students to learn to control their negative statements and temper, or do they rely on you to control them?
8. Do you help students to include everybody in the activities so that they can do this on their own?
9. Do you give students opportunities to work independently and on their own goals?
10. Do your students have a voice in evaluating each lesson and solving problems that arise?
11. Do your students have opportunities to assume meaningful leadership roles such as teaching and coaching?
12. Do you place some emphasis on transferring the levels from your class to their lives outside physical education?
13. Do your students leave your program understanding what taking responsibility means and how it applies to them?

Adapted, by permission, from D. Hellison, 2000, Youth development and physical activity *(Champaign, IL: Human Kinetics), 45-46.*

From Teaching Responsibility Through Physical Education, Second Edition by Don Hellison, 2003, Champaign, IL: Human Kinetics.

teacher survey supported my impression, it also showed that some of the teachers who started with classroom management eventually loosened their direct teaching style and changed the way they taught and related to kids, which they attributed to TPSR.

TPSR is not a management system but a way of teaching, or a "way of being" as Nick Forsberg put it (thanks to Nick for this comment). Sure, TPSR was and continues to be developed with inner-city and so-called at-risk kids who bring a host of problems into the gym, and yes, students do become more respectful as a result of

TPSR (Hellison and Walsh 2002). But focusing only on this part is like trying to sit on a one-legged chair. The TPSR questionnaire will help you determine whether this approach is right for you.

The TPSR questionnaire will help you check your compatibility with both the levels of responsibility and the four themes. Here are the four themes and the questionnaire items that ask about them:

- Integration of responsibility with the physical activity lesson: questions 6, 7, 8, 9, 11.
- Empowerment: questions 4, 5, 6, 7, 8, 9, 10, 11, 12.
- Teacher-student relationship: questions 1, 2, 3, 4, 5.
- Transfer outside the gym: questions 12, 13.

SEQUENTIAL STAGES

One cautionary note in taking the TPSR questionnaire is that the 13 questions represent a robust version of TPSR as indicated by the item analysis of the four TPSR themes. This is not a beginner's version. Although sitting on a one-legged chair doesn't work very well, you can't build the whole chair right away either. You need to envision the TPSR implementation process as a series of sequential stages toward the complete model as described in chapters 2 through 8. You take a step, evaluate it (ah, self-reflection again), tinker with it if needed, and move on to steps two, three, and so on. During this process, focus primarily on the task at hand, doing your current step in the progression as effectively as you can. Keep in mind that this is only one stage in a developmental process and that more development lies ahead.

If you are able to outlast external and often systemic obstacles such as criticism from kids or colleagues or parents, administration policies, and curriculum mandates, you will gradually find that your teaching, which has no doubt been harder since adopting TPSR, will become easier than it was before TPSR, at least in some ways. You will gain that benefit because TPSR is a less adversarial way to deal with students and because as they begin to learn how to work independently, help each other, and take on small leadership roles, you will be freer to work with the kids who are "responsibility challenged" and help those who need a little push to become more self-directed or caring.

So what are these steps that I'm referring to? Some suggestions are coming up, but they are just that—suggestions. You need to create your own steps (ah, empowerment).

If you get stuck in an early step, it may be because you have made about all the changes you can make and still survive in the system. But you may also get stuck because you have become comfortable and don't relish more disruption of your comfort zone. My advice is the same advice I'm still giving myself: When I stop refining and digging deeper into TPSR, I'm going to quit teaching kids (or when I overhear the first kid say, "Who's this old codger anyway?").

Taking Your First Steps

The easiest way to begin is to change something that will not disrupt your current curriculum too much and will only minimally change the instructional strategies you are using (or, in the case of new teachers, the curriculum and instructional strategies you've been taught to use). If this change works, you can take additional steps. If the change doesn't work, little is lost. To reduce the risk further, you can single out one class for a TPSR trial. If it works better than what you are now doing, you will likely start doing it in other classes. If the trial fails, you can go back to your old ways. Of the PE teachers who have chosen to work with one class, some have selected their most disruptive class, figuring they have little to lose. Others have started with one of their best-behaved classes, reasoning that if it doesn't work there it won't work anywhere.

If you do change your teaching practice in any way, be sure to give the change enough time to succeed or fail on its own merits. Remember, both you and your students will be new at this; you can't expect either them or yourself to pull off a smooth transition from old to new ways. My advice on outlasting the critics and bureaucracy applies here: Outlast the initial struggle and the inevitable mistakes.

Introducing the Beginning Levels

Probably the least disruptive strategy is to start with Levels I and II. That way, you start with two guidelines common to many teachers—respect for others and participation in the lesson. Also, by starting with the first two levels, you don't need to change your practice to accommodate independent work or helping roles. You can post the levels and use awareness talks to introduce Levels I and II and their relevance for an upcoming lesson or for specific incidents in class. If nothing else, the levels give you a vocabulary and a progression for talking with students about taking responsibility for not abusing others and for participating in class. They provide a framework that everyone can understand for dealing with negative attitudes, conflicts, and nonparticipation that arise with one student, between two students, or in a game. Teaching practices that don't permit students to take responsibility obviously will hinder development of personal and social responsibility, but awareness is a beginning.

Keep your awareness talks brief. Long-windedness is typical of beginning teachers and sometimes veterans as well. Also, check your students' body language—are eyes rolling?—to better recognize whether they are understanding or buying in to your message. Use language your kids understand and can relate to. "Respect" might work for Level I, but "self-control" might be better. Maybe another word is better yet. Or ask the kids what words they would use. One of Missy Parker's students suggested "Just do it" for Level III when that Nike slogan was popular.

Fran Zavacky (1997, 30), an elementary school PE teacher in Charlottesville, Virginia, together with her students, her teaching partner, and his students

> wrote descriptions stating what each level would look like in the physical education setting. Students accepted the descriptions because they resulted from collaboration between students and teachers. The discussions involved in developing the descriptions helped create an environment where students had the courage to try new things without worrying about their peers' reactions. The students began to see how they could fit in and still succeed at their individual developmental levels. During the school year, we watched the students grow into cooperative, caring young people who challenged themselves more than we as teachers could have done, and who supported each other in ways we did not anticipate.

In a variation of Fran's process, you might consider having your students suggest some respect rules for the class. If you ask them to tell you things they don't want done to themselves, you can use some of their suggestions for Level I.

Don't be afraid to be creative. Aleita Hass-Holcombe has used a tape recorder in the corner of the gym so that her children can go over and listen to the latest awareness talk message from the secret agent (thanks to Aleita for this example)!

Because many teachers use the cumulative levels, you could post all the cumulative levels but emphasize Levels I and II first. In this case you will need to teach your students the difference between Level Zero and Level I, being abusive or disruptive versus being under control, and between I and II, being under control versus participating under control.

Adding Reflection Time

After awareness talks are under way, adding a brief reflection time at the end of every class will reinforce the awareness talks but more important will involve your students in applying the levels to themselves. It's one thing to hear your teacher saying something like "I want you to take more responsibility for controlling what you say to others." It is quite another to have to show everyone how well you controlled what you said to others during the lesson. A simple show of hands (yes or no) for Levels I and II or even pointing their thumbs up (yes), sideways (sort of), and down (no) is quick and easy to teach and learn.

Notice how your students evaluate themselves in reflection time by requesting that they keep their hands up or thumbs pointed until you can look at everyone. Obtain impressions of the entire group's assessment of themselves for each level as well as a cursory sense of how individuals rated themselves in relation to your observations in class.

Adding Group Meetings

Group meetings after the physical activity lesson can be added occasionally. These can be brief. For example, you might ask students to choose an emergency plan for a game from among options you offer them or ask them to share what they liked or disliked about class that day. Even if only two students who volunteer are called on, you are acknowledging their voices in the class process.

Running an effective group meeting takes more skill than conducting an awareness talk or reflection time, although all these strategies require some skills. Listen to your students in group meetings. Pay attention to their comments on the class and each other so that you can respond appropriately and make changes if you think they would improve the class.

Adding Levels

Somewhere in this process, you need to begin to add Levels III and IV. You can't do much with Level III or IV unless your students have opportunities to practice them. Strategies that introduce a moderate version of empowerment, such as stations for Level III and reciprocal coaching for Level IV, permit you to begin talking about Levels III and IV (see the next section). As you take more steps in the implementation process, the strategies you use will advance as well.

Level V can wait until at least some of your students show they can handle the first four levels reasonably well. Transfer outside the gym is difficult because the climate is usually much less supportive. Students therefore need successful experiences with the levels in class first.

Adding Self-Grading

You can tiptoe into self-grading by asking students to grade themselves on one of their responsibilities (that is, one of the levels) along with a brief (one sentence) explanation or rationale. You only need to tell them you'll consider their self-grade when you grade them. In fact, some of their decisions and arguments may influence you.

INTEGRATION OF RESPONSIBILITY INTO THE PHYSICAL ACTIVITY LESSON

According to most teachers, changing your physical activity lesson is the most difficult part of implementing TPSR. That's because

- unlike the physical activity lesson, the awareness talk, group meeting, and reflection time are add-ons rather than something you've been doing that you need to change;
- the awareness talk, group meeting, and reflection time are also about talking and listening, not action, and therefore you can more easily control them;
- integrating responsibility into the activity lesson requires that you change practices you may have been doing for some time and probably have confidence in; and
- integration also requires that you have the knowledge and pedagogical skills to teach the physical activity; the knowledge, pedagogical skills, and qualities to teach responsibility (chapters 2-8); and the ability to integrate the two.

Beginning Strategies for the Physical Activity Lesson

I therefore recommend that you tiptoe into the integration of responsibility with the activity you are teaching. You can integrate some strategies without disrupting the curriculum:

- Introduce inclusion activities and rules (for example, in floor hockey, everyone must touch the puck before the team shoots).
- If you already use stations, introduce self-paced challenges, such as an individualized progression of soccer kicking and trapping activities, at the stations.
- Reciprocal coaching is easy to work into most motor-skill drills by partnering students. You demonstrate three or so skill cues and give them a specific task, such as to take five shots at the basket. Assign one as the first coach (the person with the ball or the person closest to the door) and charge him or her with observing the partner and giving feedback on the cues. The students then switch coach-player roles and get together afterward to tell each other how they coached (rather than how they played).

Physical Activity Lesson Strategies for Discipline and Motivation Problems

Some strategies may be useful because they meet an immediate need you have:

- You could install a talking bench for arguments between two students, although you will have to accompany the first few pairs to the bench and teach them how to talk to each other about the problem. You should instruct them to come to you and tell you it's over before they return to the game.

- DeLine's "no plan, no play" strategy could be effective for abusive game players, or you could use the sit-out progression; both are described in chapter 6.

- Task modification—"Do as many sit-ups as you can," "Get close enough to the goal (target) so you can be successful, then back up"—might improve your students' motivation in drills.

Advanced Strategies for the Physical Activity Lesson

Some strategies can wait until you become more confident or students become comfortable and somewhat competent at the first steps in taking responsibility:

- You can use the accordion principle occasionally for the entire group, but more often you will use it for individuals or small groups when you entrust students to choose from some options, officiate their own games, take on leadership roles, or assume other responsibilities described in past chapters. Many such strategies can be employed in small steps or in advanced applications of TPSR.

- When you are going to play a game, you could set up a choice of games—for example, competitive and recreational, or competitive and cooperative, or game play versus practice, perhaps using task cards for the practice. This approach will require a brief talk beforehand about how to choose and a brief reflection time afterward to ask students whether their choice worked for them.

JUMPING STEPS

Some teachers have deviated markedly from this progression. Barrie Gordon of Massey University College of Education in Palmerston North, New Zealand, reported that a local middle school PE teacher, with Barrie's help, implemented TPSR and within three months had her students choosing their own fitness activities in the first 15 minutes of class. In a surprise move, one of the two classes in which she implemented TPSR had voted to come in for physical education on a designated day off school (thanks to Barrie for this example)!

Jeff Walsh (Hellison 1983) took a two-hour workshop, then called me about three months later to say that he thought he had everything I talked about in place with his kids. And he did! Matt Smith (1990) started his junior high school students with awareness talks and then jumped to the development of personal plans for Level III time. He then added reflection time and group meetings. Chicago-area elementary PE teacher Kathy Woyner introduced awareness talks, reflection time, and self-grading at the same time in her upper elementary PE classes (thanks to Kathy for this example).

ADVANCED STEPS

After getting started, you begin to have more choices. As I've argued, you can continue to advance your understanding and practice of TPSR for a long time, maybe for the rest of your career. The strategy suggestions in chapters 4, 5, 6, and 8 offer a buffet of choices. Select and add carefully, taking stock along the way to be certain that the TPSR practices you've already established don't drop off your agenda (unless you are substituting an advanced strategy). Here are a couple of ideas to loosen your thinking.

The traditional two- or three-week unit has been criticized for emphasizing exposure over improvement (Siedentop 1991). To address this problem, you could add a Level III day near the end of the unit in which students choose to work on selected skills in the unit or skills from previous units or even on fitness activities. At a high school in Portland, Oregon, Liz Nixon and I added a Level III week after every third unit. Students could choose to improve their skills or fitness in one of the three unit activities or from previous units. We placed students not willing or able to handle such independence

---

KidQuotes

"If you want to go around musty [without a shower], it's your choice."—High school freshman

"It helped me believe in myself."—Seventh grader

"I improved as a person because any other time I wouldn't want girls on my team."—Sixth grader

in a teacher-directed group and gave them a one-week unit such as a different activity, fitness, or some advanced skills. For this to work, you should offer the teacher-directed unit to everyone—some will want to do it if the activities are attractive—and "invite" those who haven't proven themselves able to do Level III work (such as "So far you haven't been able to be responsible on your own, so you'll have to be with me until you're ready to take on some responsibility"). You should also "invite" those who have not demonstrated the ability to handle their independence during the week. Level IV student leaders can help monitor the Level III activities while you take charge of the teacher-directed group. Sometimes an advanced student leader can assume this responsibility.

Such scheduling depends on the teaching station and available equipment, but creativity also helps. I've conducted volleyball drills in the wrestling room and volleyball and martial-arts stations in the weight room.

A related approach is to select one physical activity as the focus activity for the year or semester. Each week, students develop further in the focus-activity skills or fitness. Fitness is a common theme, but you or your students could choose a sport, creating a modified version of sport education (Siedentop 1994). I have had some success in using volleyball, to the point that students begin to see themselves as a team rather than a class.

You might also make use of time before class for Level III. This way students can work on any of the activities that have been introduced while you take roll, help kids with their personal plans, and conduct counseling time. If things are going well, this Level III time can extend into the lesson.

TEACHING AS A SUBVERSIVE ACTIVITY

Making program changes in school physical education is no easy task. You usually have to do it without much support, sometimes with some opposition, and always amid a hundred other pressing duties and responsibilities. Therefore, your motivation has to be high just to get started. In some schools, innovative teaching is treated as a subversive activity. For example, if you are new, be careful about sharing your approach with other teachers. They may not share your enthusiasm and may say things like "We've tried that before" or "You'll learn better eventually." The motivation for these rebuffs can take many forms, including jealousy or the fear that they may be asked to do something new. Staff and administration won't spend much time checking on what you're doing unless they have reason to suspect that something weird is going on in your gym. If your kids like TPSR, they can certainly tell their parents about it, but if your kids talk to other students, who in turn complain to their teachers about not being given choices and so on, look out!

Telling parents can sometimes work wonders. Walt Kelly, a high school physical education teacher in Bozeman, Montana, was called into the principal's office to discuss what he was doing in PE. Walt prepared himself for a reprimand, but the principal just wanted to know what he was doing with responsibility. It seems that the parents had been calling the principal to share their excitement about what their kids were learning from Walt (thanks to Walt for this example)! Jeff Walsh's principal, a former coach and physical education teacher, pressured him to go back to traditional PE. When Jeff told his kids about the principal's request, they groaned and asked what they could do about it. Jeff replied, "Nothing, unless you want to tell your parents." The next day the principal came to see Jeff and said, "Jeff, we could have worked it out!" He left Jeff alone after that (thanks to Jeff for this example).

Class size is an obstacle to doing TPSR effectively. Jeff Walsh knew better than to argue with his school district about how his large classes interfered with his curriculum goals. Instead, he went to his principal (the same guy) and argued that he needed class-size reductions for safety reasons. After a month had passed with no action, he wrote the school district. They came out, observed, and told the principal to cut the class size! (Good thing Jeff was tenured!)

The vice-principal of a large high school told Bill White and me that he had no money to pay for some videos of skills being correctly performed, which we needed to individualize our classes. So we wrote a proposal for a small state grant for classroom improvements. We didn't get the grant, but when the vice-principal read a copy of the letter, he called us in and said he had no idea that we were teaching responsibility and honoring individuality, something he as a fat kid never got. He gave us the money.

If you stay in the mainstream you won't need to confront most of these problems. But if you try to implement TPSR or some other departure from business as usual, be prepared to weather the storm. You may be pleasantly surprised by the support you get, especially if you work with truly student-centered administrators and teachers, but it doesn't hurt to anticipate problems that usually accompany the implementation of innovative practices.

Even if the staff is supportive, your kids may not be receptive. The longer they have been doing physical education a different way, especially if they were successful or having fun, the more difficult it will be for them to adapt to change. Taking small steps enables both you and your students to adjust to change. One of the teacher qualities discussed in chapter 8, persistence, or what I call outlasting your kids, is especially helpful when your students balk at change. Of course, you need to accompany your persistence with listening and observing, sizing up the situation, and making adjustments. The goal, however, remains the same: to help kids become more responsible.

Take-Aways

Here are some things from this chapter that you might consider taking with you:

- Because TPSR is, at its heart, a way of teaching, the first step in getting started is to be certain that you want to get started! The TPSR teacher questionnaire can help, as long as you understand that the statements describe an ideal version of TPSR, a distant vision for most of us. That's OK, because implementation is a gradual progression toward the ideal version of TPSR.

- The first steps usually involve introduction of Levels I and II in a brief awareness talk, followed soon after by a brief reflection time at the end of the lesson.

- Subsequent steps involve gradually implementing the other levels and a group meeting, and eventually introducing responsibility strategies during the physical activity lesson.

- Sometimes you must treat TPSR as a subversive activity because your various stakeholders—other teachers, administrators, parents, and even your students—may find these ideas too radical. In these instances, let your actions speak for you rather than try to explain your way of teaching to those who may be hostile to your ideas. On the other hand, parents can be effective advocates of your program if they notice positive changes in their son or daughter (that is, Level V, transfer outside the gym).

Chapter 10

PROGRAMS TO SUPPLEMENT IN-SCHOOL PHYSICAL EDUCATION

The smallest act of mercy, even an encouraging word, can save a life. —Isaac Bashevis Singer

Daryl Siedentop (1992) admonished us to "think differently" about PE curriculum planning. One way to do that is to use TPSR or other alternative curriculum-instruction models. You may need to think differently in other ways as well because required in-school physical education usually involves lots of kids and many classes, making full implementation of TPSR difficult. As a result, some, perhaps many, students often remain "responsibility challenged."

In-school physical education, after-school organized sport, recess, and intramurals are the typical school structures for physical activity programs. You may want to think differently by creating new structures. For example, Siedentop suggested a fitness center that students could use at different times, including before and after school. Physical education teachers have created jogging clubs complete with maps to track students' miles. The following alternative TPSR structures have been implemented in schools:

- Cross-age teaching and leadership programs
- Voluntary by-invitation clubs that meet before or after school or during lunch
- A responsibility-based fitness center

You might also be able to utilize traditional school structures to reinforce your TPSR message. For example, some schools have extended

TPSR by adopting it in the classroom, on the playground and at recess, in organized sport programs after school, and even schoolwide.

CROSS-AGE TEACHING AND LEADERSHIP

Cross-age teaching and leadership has already been described as both a Level IV and V experience (in chapter 5). Although it presents one more administrative headache, arranging for older students already experienced in TPSR who are able and willing to work with younger kids is a way to assist your more responsibility-challenged younger students, while at the same time giving cross-age leaders a chance to practice Level IV and experience Level V. (Regrettably, the term *leader,* while overused, generally is more popular among students than the term *teacher.*) (See Hellison, Cutforth, Kallusky, Martinek, Parker, and Stiehl 2000 for an extended discussion of cross-age teaching.)

Ages of Cross-Age Leaders

Older students can be fourth and fifth graders working with first, second, and third graders. Or they can be eighth or ninth graders either working with sixth or seventh graders in their school or traveling to the elementary school to work with younger kids. High school juniors and seniors can work with younger high school students or travel to the junior high (or middle school) or elementary school to assist there. In all these situations, you must be able to trust the cross-age leaders to take on the Level IV responsibilities (see chapters 3 and 5).

In addition, some responsibility-challenged older students respond to being given leadership responsibilities. In a low-income minority community in Denver, Nick Cutforth's (2000) cross-age leaders were junior high students initially selected for his elementary program based on their poor disciplinary record. They came back weekly to their old elementary school as program teaching assistants. Terry Cooper had some of her most responsibility-challenged sixth graders teach first graders, and she reported that they were great teachers (thanks to Terry for this example)! I have had success with supposedly responsibility-challenged alternative high school students teaching younger kids in an elementary school as well as with inner-city students grade 7 through 12 teaching 10-year-olds from a different neighborhood.

Training for Cross-Age Teaching

Preparing students to become cross-age teachers creates yet another administrative headache: finding the time and energy to conduct mini-preservice teaching sessions. Here are some ways I have tried to prepare cross-age teachers:

- Peer teaching and coaching, being integral parts of TPSR, can help prepare students for working with younger kids, especially if accompanied by reflection on the experience.

- You can have some of your students take turns conducting the awareness talk and, with help, the group meeting and reflection time for their class. They can volunteer for these assignments, or you can invite students who demonstrate leadership potential. I've found that inviting individual students before class or during a previous class allows them time to prepare mentally.

- Reciprocal coaching (see chapter 5) can be extended so that students demonstrate the skills to each other, point out important cues, observe, and give feedback.

- You can develop a unit in teaching or leadership so that your students can practice teaching lessons that they will use with younger kids. If you videotape them teaching, they will enjoy watching themselves in action and you can add instructional tips.

Tom Martinek (Martinek and Schilling 2002) uses this progression for his students:

1. Students still deal with personal needs.
2. Students work on teaching skills, such as organizing and managing other kids and giving feedback.
3. Students reflect on their teaching and how it has influenced their personal growth and knowledge about other kids.
4. Students teach with compassion and teach others to be compassionate.

COACHING CLUBS

I created my first coaching club over a decade ago as an alternative structure for the implementation of TPSR. The club still operates before school one or two days a week. Several of us conduct similar extended day clubs, which we described recently in some detail (Hellison et al. 2000). Although we have done this work in community youth agency settings, our most successful experiences have been in schools before and after school (Walsh 2002) or, in Mike DeBusk's case (DeBusk and Hellison 1989) at lunchtime. Although none of us is a full-time PE teacher, some PE teachers—notably Jim Joseph in New Albany, Ohio, and April Rodgers near Washington, D.C.—run after-school coaching clubs for small groups of responsibility-challenged students.

What's in a Name?

TPSR becomes more visible to the kids, parents, administrators, and other teachers by calling it a coaching club rather than a soccer club (or whatever activity you are doing). Although the term *coaching* conjures up a variety of images, some of which are not too positive, it does convey to everyone that the club is doing something more than learning and playing a sport or other physical activity. We use it to indicate that the emphasis is on learning how to help others and become a leader.

The name *coaching club* refers to sport, although fitness, adventure education, martial arts, tumbling, and sports in general have also been used. Any activity will work. The key is to choose something that will attract the kids you want in the club. Basketball is a shoo-in where I work, and the kids get up an hour early to come.

Sometimes it helps to have the activity name in the title to attract kids. For example, our martial-arts program is called the martial-arts leadership club, indicating the activity but also the focus on going beyond the activity.

Advantages

Creating a coaching club offers several advantages:

- You can give responsibility-challenged students more attention and more practice at taking responsibility by keeping club membership small, maybe 10 or 12 unless you have help from cross-age leaders, university students, or aides. Class size is your call.

- Kids have something meaningful to belong to—a club in which they have a voice, can make decisions, and eventually become leaders.

- As long as the space is available, you can create your own schedule, including how many days the club meets each week and for how long. We run several one-day-a-week clubs that appear to have a positive effect on the kids (Hellison et al. 2000).

- You can invite selected students to attend, thereby not creating resentment among students who are ordered to attend a mandatory experience (such as in-school physical education).

If the students like the activity, they are likely to show up and check it out. Recently, one boy said to the vice-principal who makes all the referrals for my coaching club, "How bad do you have to be to get in that club?!!"

• You can relax some of the usual PE rules such as uniforms, and you don't need large-class management routines such as squads. Because attendance is voluntary, it's not essential to get it right. You may want to keep track of who shows up (their responsibility!), but you can probably do it by memory when the club is over.

Issues

You may not have the time or energy to take on another responsibility. Because the coaching club is an alternative structure, getting strong administrative support is difficult, especially compared with the support you can normally expect for interschool organized sport or intramurals. You have to decide whether it's worth the effort to set aside 40 minutes or so once a week to help kids who struggle with taking responsibility, and whether you have the energy to organize and conduct such a program. If you are near a university, you may be able to find a university student to become a coaching-club intern. If the intern is successful, he or she may be able to take over the club's leadership, freeing you from this extra duty. My colleagues and I have had quite a bit of success using this approach (Hellison et al. 2000).

Another issue is finding a teaching station to run your club if the gym is occupied by other activities. You may be able to improvise. I've conducted a martial-arts coaching club on a stage with staggering temperatures from the stage lights, and we currently teach the same program in a classroom after school. I've also taught volleyball in the wrestling room. A key criterion for exemplary extended-day programs is to "provide courageous and persistent leadership in the face of systemic obstacles" (Hellison et al. 2000, 32).

KidQuotes

"How bad do I have to be to get into the coaching club?"—Fifth grader

"Don helped me. Now I'm helping him [teach younger kids]."—High school junior

"What if them little kids don't listen to us?"—Seventh grader

Although you want to select an activity that is likely to attract your responsibility-challenged students, they may be interested in an activity in which you possess little skill or knowledge—for example, hacky-sack. Of course, you can learn. Better yet, if you can be a bit vulnerable (see chapter 7), you can have your kids teach you, a situation that provides them an authentic Level IV experience.

Sample Coaching-Club Lesson

Because coaching clubs are so varied in content, it is impossible to offer a generic coaching-club lesson plan. Here is a team-sport lesson plan based on the basketball and soccer coaching clubs we conduct in Chicago (for descriptions of a sport-fitness club and a martial arts club, see Hellison et al. 2000).

- You have ample time for counseling and free play at the beginning of the lesson. With fewer students, you can talk with most or all the students every session if some of these "talks" are simple exchanges. Free play gives students a chance to practice their skills and, if you work on goal setting, to work on their goals. The only rule is Level I—respect others and include everyone, that is, share the balls and space!

- With fewer kids, you can sit in a circle and briefly discuss the purpose of the club. Asking students questions, listening to their input, and commenting on their contributions generally work better than minilectures by you.

- Students then get a second opportunity to work on a specific goal, which they report on during reflection time.

- While students are working on their goals (or just practicing), you meet with the coaches for the day's game. Or, if you are just getting started, you meet with the assistant coaches (you can start as head coach). Or, you can hold this meeting before the awareness talk, allowing you to move directly from the awareness talk to team practices.

  - At first, you can give them a card on which you have written their plan for conducting a practice for their team. As they become more experienced, they can choose their own drills, the defense they will use in the game, and offensive plays.

  - The coaches also have to create fair teams with your help. They may pick sides as long as other kids aren't listening in and both coaches agree that the sides are fair.

• Because new teams are created for each lesson, rivalries don't interfere with the purpose of the club and all club members play with each other some of the time.

• You then help the coaches gather their teams and manage the practice.

• Before the game, call the coaches together and remind them that they are in charge and need to call time-outs to make adjustments and solve problems that arise.

• The game has several rules that differ from traditional sport:

> • Offense and defense are at first based on the zone, because it emphasizes passing and reduces body contact, one-on-one trash talk, and the embarrassment of making a mistake in one-on-one defense. Eventually, you introduce player-to-player defense, along with picks, two- and three-player games, posting up, and so on. Coaches choose defensive and offensive strategies from those that have been introduced.

> • The all-touch rule, which requires that everyone on the team handle the ball before the team can shoot (inclusion), is used until students understand that this is a team game and that everyone deserves to be involved. Surprisingly, the kids usually don't contest this rule, but they watch the other team carefully for violations. With the all-touch rule, players learn teamwork, how to move off the ball to get clear for a pass, and how to pass more effectively.

> • Because there are no referees, coaches and players must take responsibility for conducting a fair game.

> • Players and especially coaches can call a time-out at any time to deal with problems or discuss strategy. At first, you will need to call time-outs. Once students experience conducting time-outs on their own (with you casually observing), they will begin to call their own. When a conflict breaks out and I start toward the group, what I want to hear is, "We don't need you; we can handle it." After some practice, they don't disappoint.

> • The soft-defense rule requires that the more highly skilled players not overplay the less skilled players on the opposing team. The kids understand why this rule has been created, but during an intense game they sometimes suffer from temporary amnesia.

- You can participate in the game if teams are uneven because with a small class size you will probably have only one game going on. If you do, you can model passing the ball, moving off the ball, not fouling while defending, and so on.

- The group meeting follows the game. Again, students sit in a circle, but this time coaches (or in the beginning assistant coaches) talk first, sharing their perceptions of how practice and the game went and who made positive contributions on their team. Then any player can talk about the practice or game as long as the comments are constructive. Finally, you can share your observations. Be sure not to talk first. If you do, you will likely shut down student voices.

- Students stay in the circle for reflection time. You can address the first four levels by having students point their thumbs up, sideways, or down to indicate how they did with that level in the session. If they had time to work on individual goals, ask them to rate themselves on Level III according to whether they worked on their goal, went through the motions, or did not try at all. Because you will not be in a rush compared with the situation you have in your normal PE class, you could have students write about how they took responsibility. Of course, you will then have to read their journal entries and comment.

RESPONSIBILITY-BASED FITNESS CENTER

Compared with some other activities, fitness lends itself more to having kids take responsibility. The activities—stretching, weight training, push-ups and sit-ups, running, stationary bicycle—are easy to learn and don't require much motor-skill feedback to improve. The mechanics are simple for most students, and once they learn the basic mechanics of a push-up, bench press, or jogging, improvement will come with regular training. Moreover, fitness is easily individualized. Students start by performing the exercise correctly, record their performance, and work from there at their own pace.

The one obstacle to running a self-directed fitness center is developing students' conceptual knowledge so that they can be self-directed. They may need to learn about overload, intervals, aerobic and anaerobic training, heart-rate measurement, and body-fat reduction. Concepts posters and a brief multiple-choice (or other) test to screen students for the threshold knowledge necessary to work on their own is one simple way to deal with this issue. This process has the additional benefit of being self-directed, so that students must learn the concepts on their own and schedule their test taking. If necessary, you can issue cards authorizing students who have passed the test to be on their own in the fitness center.

Despite these advantages, a teacher must monitor students who go to the center. Unless you can find a university student interested in working individually with kids on fitness, you need to have the time and energy to take this on yourself.

Students who are willing and able to take on leadership responsibilities can, with some training or past experience, assist you in the center. Students who can manage only Levels I and II would require active supervision if they are to be allowed in the center.

At Rock Springs High School in Wyoming, Leslie Lambert and Paul Grube (1988) created such a center. Because they wanted to nurture students toward more decision making and self-management, they integrated TPSR into the activities of the center. As a result, "participation has increased, most notably in the students' feelings of responsibility for their learning and class involvement" (p. 72).

TPSR IN THE CLASSROOM

TPSR has been implemented here and there in both elementary and secondary classrooms. In almost all cases, the PE teacher's implementation of TPSR and the results he or she was getting prompted other teachers to inquire about it and request help in trying some of the ideas in their classrooms.

Classroom Applications

Most often, the levels are posted, sometimes with students doing the artwork, sometimes with considerable creativity. For example, Vicki Jorgensen, an elementary music teacher in Ashland, Oregon (who learned of the levels from the school's physical education teacher, Keith Kimball), created a four-color rainbow, with one color for each level. She called it "Put a rainbow in your life!" and the idea spread to most of the classrooms in the school. Teachers in Tom Martinek's elementary school used selected Calvin and Hobbes cartoons to illustrate each of the levels (thanks to Vicki and Tom for these examples).

Teachers have also modified TPSR strategies for use in the classroom. Steve Hoy, teaching a sixth-grade class in Billings, Montana, used the cumulative levels along with the talking bench (out in the hall) and a Level Zero table where students could separate themselves from the their classmates to cool off and make a plan to improve. He reported that TPSR has helped his kids learn how to manage themselves (thanks to Steve for this example).

One high school math teacher reported some success giving his students the choice of learning content cooperatively, competitively, or individually. Traditionally, students have been in competitive contexts—who has the best test score, who has the right answer in class—but recently both specific cooperative learning and individualized instruction strategies have been made available to teachers. From a TPSR perspective, students should probably be exposed to all three learning processes but eventually be able to choose the one or two that work best for them.

Ray Petracek (1998), teaching all subjects to his class of grade-seven students in Regina, Saskatchewan, had his students make journal entries at the end of the day to rate themselves on the percentage of time during the day that they functioned at each of his adapted levels of responsibility:

- No control ___%
- Self-control ___%
- Involvement with effort ___%
- Self-direction ___%
- Caring for others ___%
- Responsible leadership ___%

Every Monday morning Ray assisted his students in setting class goals for the week. He also kept track of incidence of not being prepared for class, disrespect for his right to teach, disrespect for others' right to learn, and issuing a put-down or threat. He used these data to give feedback to his students, to discuss the problems, and to make plans to solve them. Finally, he gave them the following written assignment from time to time: "Describe a scenario or issue so that the six levels of responsibility are displayed. For the scenario, identify setting, characters, and the issue" (Petracek 1998).

Health Education Applications

Because some physical education teachers also teach health education, those who use TPSR sometimes experiment with it in health education. In addition, TPSR addresses a key issue in health education: taking responsibility for one's physical, emotional, and social health. Because of these factors, many of the classroom applications have been in health education.

Bill White may have been the first to implement TPSR in health education. His Portland, Oregon, high school health education program was a semester course that included a number of short units, such as nutrition, drug education, sex education, and so on. White began the course with a mental health unit that featured the levels.

Through awareness talks, discussions (similar to group meetings), and reflection time, he encouraged students to see the relevance of the levels for their lives both in and out of school. He focused on the necessity of respect in social relations, the importance of participation and effort in learning or improving anything, the relevance of self-direction for the many choices students face on a daily basis, the need to be cared for and helped, and the benefit of offering these things to others. After this initial unit, the levels were applied to subsequent units, so that students were confronted with issues of self-control, self-direction (making personal decisions), and caring about others in drug and sex education, in nutrition decisions, even in driver education (thanks to Bill for this example).

Chris Hare (1998), a high school health education teacher in a Chicago suburb, was aware that he was just "spitting out information," but he knew that his students needed to learn to make health-related decisions for themselves, based on their needs and interests as long as no one was adversely affected. As a result, he created his own levels of responsibility for his classes. His levels focused on the climate he was trying to establish to teach health education in an empowering way:

- I: Self-responsibility
  - Effort on homework
  - Coming to class prepared with the materials they need
- II: Self-control
  - Right to be included in class discussions, to make a positive contribution to class
  - Right to peaceful conflict resolution in class discussions
- III: Self-direction
  - Participation in class, sharing one's thoughts
  - Becoming independent thinkers, not subject to peer pressure
- IV: Out of the classroom
  - Health education applications in life
  - Caring about and helping others (for example, helping one's family develop a fire-escape plan)
- V: Self-actualization
  - Setting long-term goals
  - Reaching self-fulfillment and one's potential

In her wellness course, Mary Sinclair uses the levels to help students reflect on personal and social wellness. Students score themselves on a 1 to 10 scale on each level, and Sinclair asks them to make open-ended written comments. Form 10.1 shows how Sinclair redefined the levels to represent wellness attitudes, values, and behaviors.

Leslie McBride and I taught health education and physical education as one course to high school students using TPSR as the framework (Hellison and McBride 1986). We introduced physical, emotional, and social health concepts in a format similar to awareness talks in the classroom. The students then went to the gym to experience these concepts. Classroom group meetings and reflection time for evaluating the effect of the experience on their health followed. The class discussed student participation in community action projects as outgrowths of these experiences.

TPSR on the *Playground* and at *Recess*

Curt Hinson adapted TPSR for the playground and recess. Hinson wrote that his interest began this way:

> When I tried to place too much control over them I ended up in a power struggle with kids who didn't know how to act appropriately. That's when I went in search of a method that could help me to teach students to be self-responsible. (Hinson 2001, 63)

Hinson adapted the levels of responsibility by reducing the five levels to three "levels of behavior": unacceptable (for example, not following directions, arguing, hitting or pushing), acceptable (for example, following directions, taking care of equipment, respecting others), and outstanding (for example, cooperating with others, helping others, being a role model). Posters of these levels were placed where kids could see them regularly, such as the cafeteria and classrooms, and, when possible, they were reminded of the levels before they went to the playground—for example, by asking them for examples of the levels.

Once kids understood the levels, they could make choices about how they want to be on the playground. The key to Hinson's approach is for students to choose their behaviors rather than for adults to tell them what to do. Ideally, unacceptable behaviors will not make them popular playmates, but they may need some assistance to figure that out. The playground supervisor's job is to help students who are behaving unacceptably to identify their level of behavior, and, if it is unacceptable, to change it on their own. Some children, however, may need help to solve a particular problem, such as an argument, or to understand how they can change to acceptable and outstanding behaviors. "The supervisor should avoid . . . telling

Form 10.1

Wellness Responsibility Levels

How would you grade yourself on self-responsibility for your wellness? Using the responsibility levels, rate yourself by circling the number you feel best represents your effort at each of the levels. Discuss your self-evaluation below by elaborating and using examples to support your self-perceptions.

	Low									**High**

0-I: Self-control and respect   1   2   3   4   5   6   7   8   9   10

> 0: Abusive, destructive health behavior. No ownership of own health.
>
> I: Minimal investment in personal wellness. Lack of awareness about personal needs and skills. Health behaviors not unhealthy but not necessarily constructive.

II: Participation and effort   1   2   3   4   5   6   7   8   9   10

> Willing to put effort into own wellness. Disciplined. Open to ideas and experiences. Ready to risk change. Ready to develop self-awareness. Self-knowledge (first connection between class and personal wellness).

III: Self-direction   1   2   3   4   5   6   7   8   9   10

> Accepting responsibility for all aspects of own health. Owning goals and problems. Using skills of "response-ability" to internalize and work problems out. Self-initiated goal setting and self-evaluation. High level of personal awareness.

IV: Helping others   1   2   3   4   5   6   7   8   9   10

> Role model for wellness. Help others with their wellness.

From *Teaching Responsibility Through Physical Education,* Second Edition *by Don Hellison, 2003, Champaign, IL: Human Kinetics.*

children what to do. . . . Making suggestions is fine, but let the children make the final choice" (Hinson 2001).

Kids who blame others for what is happening don't understand self-responsibility. They may need some help to shift their thinking to what they need to do rather than what others are doing. As a last resort, the supervisor can step in and solve the problem. After other options have been attempted and a child's behavior is still unacceptable, removing the child from recess may be necessary.

TPSR in Organized Sport

Putting TPSR into practice in organized sport (or interscholastic athletics) is in some ways a formidable undertaking. As I noted in chapter 1, character development rhetoric is an integral part of organized sport, although whether sport truly builds character is a matter of debate. These programs, however, do provide supervised places for kids during their free time and they require kids to make commitments. Organized sport has great appeal in our culture; it is a magnet for kids, who tend to develop strong ties to the sport and their teams.

Then why is putting TPSR into practice in organized sport so difficult? The primary problem is the influence of the professional sport model that has trickled all the way down to programs for kids. Most organized sport programs, sometimes even at the T-ball level, try to replicate the winning-is-everything, elitist, spectator-driven orientation of the big-time sport model. Despite attempts to humanize sport for kids, including a number of rule modifications, too many coaches and too many parents value winning over participation, over fair play, over personal and social development. And too many coaches believe in their own authority rather than in sharing power with their players. In the inner city, the myth of playing in the NBA too often goes unanalyzed. Coaches even intentionally use it as a motivator. I am always amazed when I see professionals trained in psychological therapy or special education leave their training on the sidelines when they become coaches. In short, the cultural appeal of organized sport has its dark side.

Nevertheless, TPSR has been implemented in organized sport. Moreover, former professional basketball player Nikos Georgiadis argued that the motor elite sorely need this perspective, because they are victims of the professional sport model and its values (thanks to Nikos for this example). The next section describes three examples.

Walt Kelly, a veteran football coach, and Cynthia Luebbe began to use TPSR in their high school classes in Bozeman, Montana. Kelly then decided to try out these ideas in football. He reconceptualized the levels as shown in table 10.1 so that being a player meant being at Level II. Level I meant that the player was working on the qualities needed to become a player. At Levels III and IV the concepts of self-direction and coaching were added. He taught these levels to his players in awareness talks and required that they do self-evaluations during a scheduled reflection time at the end of practice. This self-evaluation consisted of written comments for each level, followed by written feedback from Kelly.

Table 10.1   Walt Kelly's Football Team Levels of Responsibility

Level	Name	Description
I	Preplayer	The first and foremost goal is to respect the rights and feelings of teammates, opponents, coaches, officials, and spectators by using self-control (rather than coach control). This includes controlling one's abusive behavior, such as put-downs and arrogance, and disruptive behavior, such as interfering with practice. It also includes negotiating differences. This is a prerequisite to participating on the team and requires the highest need for direct supervision.
II	Player	The second level involves becoming involved in the activities of the team, learning from failure, redefining success so that success can be experienced (e.g., improvement as success), losing oneself in the game, and having fun. Again, the goal is to shift this responsibility to the players.
III	Self-coach	The goal of the third level is to help the players manage their own development, to be their own coach. Players face a number of conflicts at this stage—between peer pressure and their own goals, between "looking good" and self-acceptance, etc. The coach's role is to help players to see these conflicts and to experiment with solutions.
IV	Coach	The goal of the fourth level is to learn how to support and help others, to extend oneself beyond one's own needs and interests, to become an assistant coach.

He also conducted group meetings in which players could share their ideas about practice, game plans, and decisions. Kelly, a former marine, reported that TPSR forced him to rethink his coaching style and to shift from issuing commands to collaborating and negotiating with his players (thanks to Walt and Cynthia for this example).

Bill White put TPSR into practice with his interscholastic wrestling and gymnastic teams in Portland, Oregon. All his senior athletes were Level IV assistant coaches; they helped run practice and coach the younger athletes. In addition, certain athletes had specific Level IV roles, such as the nutrition coach who taught everyone about healthy weight-reducing practices in wrestling. His athletes were responsible for making decisions about whether to come to practice (Level II) and, with assistance at first, what kind of workout to do (Level III). During group meetings, players decided who would start. That way, the decision of whether to come to practice became a team decision. Many of White's athletes were considered at-risk students in school. In gymnastics competitions, officials would regularly deduct points for their dress and "nongymnastics attitude." Despite this, his team took several city titles in gymnastics and placed in the top three in the state every year he coached. He coached wrestling for a shorter time, but his ideas turned around a struggling wrestling team almost immediately. The point here is not that winning is important, but that a coach who employs TPSR can win too. The Positive Coaching Alliance would call Bill a double-goal coach (thanks to Bill for this example).

Kostas Keramidas (1991) used TPSR with his junior basketball team, which plays in a highly competitive league in Greece. He reported that the TPSR approach has reduced the influence of the star system imported from the United States ("Be like Mike"), that most of his players have reached Level IV, that their reflection-time journals show they are thinking, and that their basketball skills have improved. Referees and coaches praised his team for their unselfish play and their performance. Because his team has performed so well, other coaches in the league started using reflection-time journals, not to help their players become more responsibly reflective but in the hope of improving the win-loss record of their teams!

SCHOOLWIDE ADOPTIONS OF TPSR

I have heard of a few schools that adopted some version of TPSR schoolwide. Several schools and even one school district have invited me to conduct TPSR workshops and presentations. The impetus for these invitations came from the success of one or more PE teachers using TPSR in the school or district. I approach these invitations wary of across-the-board adoptions of TPSR or any other one approach. Students would benefit from having consistency across the curriculum, especially if fully implemented in the halls, on the playground, and in extracurricular activities as well. But such adoption may force teachers to abandon some of the things that work well for them, and it substitutes a value-based approach that some teachers don't believe in. The test-score mania, which has shrunk the margins that creative teachers work in, is a perfect example. After all, developing one's own values and beliefs is not an objective, scientific exercise. Science can't prove that TPSR, or any other approach for that matter, is good for kids. It can only show whether it works. My message in this book as well as in any teacher in-service work I do with TPSR is best expressed by Hugh Prather (1972, no page number):

> And so I am left with this belief: that there are no answers, that there are only alternatives. . . . If my words affirm you, [take them in], but if they cause you to distrust your own experience, spit them out.

I also relied on this quote in introducing my first book (Hellison 1978), perhaps reflecting a lack of progress in my thinking. But I'd like to think it shows consistency in my belief that teachers can be self-directed.

Having shared my thoughts and feelings about mandatory adoptions, it may surprise you that I still accept invitations to discuss schoolwide adoption of TPSR. For starters, I share with teachers my skepticism about one size fitting all, just as I am doing with you. I also teach that buy-in of the foundational TPSR values—empowering kids to take personal and social responsibility and see whether it works in their lives, and developing the kind of teacher-student relationship that supports the transfer of these values to life—is essential. But if you buy in, you need to adapt TPSR to your own setting, kids, and style and progress by self-paced successive approximations.

In one middle school with which I was familiar, the librarian volunteered to direct the schoolwide operation of TPSR. She created ID cards that stated whether the student was at cumulative level III or IV. Students at level III could use their ID as a hall pass, go to the library on their own, and enjoy other perks. Students at Level IV were eligible to do these things as well as engage in peer mediation, peer and cross-age teaching, and similar activities. Some teachers did not buy in, but most did, and students were receptive to receiving perks (no surprise). I struggled with the behavior modification involved in such a system and with definitions of being responsible that were entirely behavioral, thereby promoting doing the right thing without necessarily valuing or believing in it. As I've already stated, however, it may well be that behavior precedes belief. I was involved in this implementation process, but given the importance of empowering the teachers as well as students in my value system, I kept my mouth shut.

Take-Aways

Here are some things from this chapter that you might consider taking with you:

- Taking responsibility is extremely challenging for some kids. Given teachers' large class size, several classes a day, and other duties, it is not surprising that some kids remain responsibility challenged at the end of the year.

- To supplement TPSR in physical education, thereby helping kids experience the message more consistently, new structures can be created—for example, coaching clubs, cross-age teaching programs, a fitness center.

- To supplement TPSR in structures already present in the school, TPSR can be implemented in classrooms, organized sport programs, and schoolwide.

EPILOGUE

Life is not important except in the impact it has on others.
—Jackie Robinson

What's worth doing is in my view the most important question that we as physical education teachers need to ask ourselves, and it's a question we need to ask periodically throughout our careers. Although rookie teachers legitimately worry about controlling their classes and veteran teachers sometimes search for new games or activities to fill three-week units, without a strong sense of purpose none of these concerns matter much in the long run.

Although wall charts of the responsibility levels have their place, TPSR is above all a way of teaching, perhaps even, as Nick Forsberg says, a way of being (thanks to Nick for this example). TPSR represents my beliefs and values, my answer to what's worth doing. As I continue to ask myself, "Is this stuff still worth doing?" I'm forced back to the drawing board again and again to reflect, rethink, reimagine. So far, TPSR has survived this process, but there are no guarantees. If you take this journey I hope that you will succeed but that you will abandon it if something comes along that in your view would work better for kids and more accurately represent the kind of contribution you want to make.

If you have gotten this far in the book, TPSR probably makes some sense to you, because your beliefs and values are similar to mine. If so, you may find it helpful to create a simplified vision of how your classes ought to look and work if they were based on TPSR:

- Your relationship with your kids
- Your lesson plan
- Integrating responsibility into your physical activity lesson
- Dealing with problems that arise
- Helping your students see how responsibility could transfer outside your class
- Your assessment procedures

KidQuotes

"What I disliked about this program is that we should have had it a long time ago."—Sixth grader

"I didn't change. I'm the same old person."—Sixth grader

"I'm very grateful he has you in his life."—Mother of high school sophomore

- Supplementary experiences for your responsibility-challenged kids

Although it will seem overwhelming for someone who hasn't taken the first step in implementing TPSR, creating your own vision does give you a map of the journey ahead, a map that you will no doubt rework as time passes. The map offers roads for taking first steps and progressively adding strategies as you begin to feel more comfortable. If things aren't working, you return to the drawing board to figure out how to fix what is going wrong or, more fundamentally, to revisit the question about what's worth doing.

That's really what this book is intended to be, a generic map for TPSR in school physical education—not a connect-the-dots, paint-the-numbers blueprint, but a map of ideas and possible strategies, a map that includes not only the roads to get there but the rationale for doing so.

Creating your own more streamlined map reduces these many ideas and suggestions to those most likely to be applicable to your kids in your setting as well as to your sense of purpose. Then you take the small steps described in chapter 9. If you're ready, let the process begin!

In case I have failed to convey the messiness of this process, I will close the same way I closed both the first edition of this book and *Beyond Balls and Bats* (1978), with a saying by Hugh Prather (1970):

Ideas are clean.
I can take them out and look at them.
They fit nicely into books.
They lead me down the narrow way
And in the morning they are there.

Ideas are straight.

But the world is round
And a messy mortal is my friend.

Come walk with me in the mud.

References

Arnold, P.J. 1988. *Education, movement and the curriculum.* London: Falmer.

Ayers, W. 1989. *The good preschool teacher: Six teachers reflect on their lives.* New York: Teachers College Press.

Banks, W.H., and C. Smith-Fee. 1989. Middle school PE: Assertiveness training. *Journal of Physical Education, Recreation and Dance* 60:90–93.

Beedy, J.P., and T. Zierk. 2000. Lessons from the field: Taking a proactive approach to developing character through sports. *CYD Journal: Community Youth Development* 3:6–13.

Benson, P.L. 1997. *All kids are our kids: What communities must do to raise caring and responsible children and adolescents.* San Francisco: Jossey-Bass.

Berman, S. 1990. Educating for social responsibility. *Educational Leadership* 48:75–80.

Boyes-Watson, C. 2001. Healing the wounds of street violence. *CYD Journal: Community Youth Development* 4:16–21.

Bredemeier, M.E. 1988. *Urban classroom portraits: Teachers who make a difference.* New York: Lang.

Bressan, E.S. 1987. Physical education and social change in South Africa. In *Proceedings of the fifth curriculum theory conference in physical education,* ed. M. Carnes and P. Stueck, 128–138. Athens, GA.

Buchanan, A.M. 1996. *Learner's and instructors' interpretations of personal and social responsibility in a sports camp.* Doctoral dissertation, Texas A&M University.

Caldas, S.J. 1994. Teen pregnancy: Why it remains a serious social, economic and education problem in the U.S. *Phi Delta Kappan* 75:402–406.

Camino, L.A. 2002. CO-SAMM: A tool to assess youth leadership. *CYD Journal: Community Youth Development* 3:39–43.

Carnegie Council on Adolescent Development. 1992. *A matter of time: Risk and opportunity in the nonschool hours.* Report of the Task Force on Youth Development and Community Programs. New York: Carnegie Corporation of New York.

Compagnone, N. 1995. Teaching responsibility to rural elementary youth: Going beyond the at-risk boundaries. *Journal of Physical Education, Recreation and Dance* 66:58–63.

Csikszentmihalyi, M., and J. McCormack. 1986. The influence of teachers. *Phi Delta Kappan* 67:415–419.

Cuban, L. 1993. The lure of curricular reform and its pitiful history. *Phi Delta Kappan* 75:182–185.

Cutforth, N. 2000. Connecting school physical education to the community through service learning. *Journal of Physical Education, Recreation and Dance* 71:39–45.

Cutforth, N., and M. Parker. 1996. Promoting affective development in physical education: The value of journal writing. *Journal of Physical Education, Recreation and Dance* 67:19–23.

DeBusk, M., and D. Hellison. 1989. Implementing a physical education self-responsibility model for delinquency-prone youth. *Journal of Teaching in Physical Education* 8:104–112.

deCharms, R. 1976. *Enhancing motivation: Change in the classroom.* New York: Irvington.

DeLine, J. 1991. Why . . . can't they get along? *Journal of Physical Education, Recreation and Dance* 62:21–26.

Delpit, L.D. 1988. The silenced dialogue: Power and pedagogy in educating other people's children. *Harvard Educational Review* 58:379–385.

Denton, D.E. 1972. *Existential reflections on teaching.* North Quincy, MA: Christopher.

Des Dixon, R.G. 1994. Future schools and how to get there from here. *Phi Delta Kappan* 75:360–365.

Dill, V.S. 1998. *A peaceable school: Cultivating a culture of non-violence.* Bloomington, IN: Phi Delta Kappan Educational Foundation.

Dreikurs, R., and V. Soltz. 1964. *Children: The challenge.* New York: Hawthorn.

Ennis, C.D., M.A. Solmon, B. Satina, S.J. Loftus, J. Mensch, and M.T. McCauley. 1999. Creating a sense of family in urban school using the "Sport for Peace" curriculum. *Research Quarterly for Exercise and Sport* 70:273–285.

Fejgin, N. 1994. Participation in high school competitive sports: A subversion of school mission or contribution to academic goals? *Sociology of Sport Journal* 11:211–230.

Foster, H.L. 1974. *Ribbin', jivin', and playin' the dozens: The unrecognized dilemma of inner city schools.* Cambridge, MA: Ballinger.

Georgiadis, N. 1990. Does basketball have to be all W's and L's? An alternative program at a residential boys' home. *Journal of Physical Education, Recreation and Dance* 61:42–43.

Gibbons, S.L., V. Ebbeck, and M.R. Weiss. 1995. Fair play for kids: Effects on the moral development of children in physical education. *Research Quarterly for Exercise and Sport* 66:247–255.

Giebink, M.P., and T.L. McKenzie. 1985. Teaching sportsmanship in physical education and recreation: An analysis of interventions and generalization effects. *Journal of Teaching in Physical Education* 4:167–177.

Glasser, W. 1965. *Reality therapy.* New York: Harper & Row.

Glasser, W. 1977. Ten steps to good discipline. *Today's Education* 66:61–63.

Goodlad, J. 1988. Studying the education of educators: Values driven inquiry. *Phi Delta Kappan* 69:105–111.

Gordon, G.L. 1999. Teacher talent and urban schools. *Phi Delta Kappan* 80:304–306.

Greene, M. 1986. Philosophy and teaching. In *The handbook of research on teaching,* 3rd ed., ed. M.C. Wittrock, 479–504. New York: Macmillan.

Gruber, J.J. 1984. Physical activity and self-esteem development in children: A meta-analysis. *American Academy of Physical Education Papers* 19:30–48.

Guthrie, J. 1982. *Be your own coach.* Portland, OR: ASIEP.

Hare, C. 1998. *Incorporation of the responsibility levels into the health curriculum.* Unpublished paper.

Hattie, J., H.W. Marsh, J.T. Neill, and G.E. Richards. 1997. Adventure education and outward bound: Out-of-class experiences that make a lasting difference. *Review of Educational Research* 67:43–87.

Hellison, D. 1978. *Beyond balls and bats: Alienated (and other) youth in the gym.* Washington, DC: AAHPER.

Hellison, D. 1983. Teaching self-responsibility (and more). *Journal of Physical Education, Recreation and Dance* 54:23, 28.

Hellison, D. 1985. *Goals and strategies for teaching physical education.* Champaign, IL: Human Kinetics.

Hellison, D., N. Cutforth, J. Kallusky, T. Martinek, M. Parker, and J. Stiehl. 2000. *Youth development and physical activity: Linking universities and communities.* Champaign, IL: Human Kinetics.

Hellison, D., and N. Georgiadis. 1992. Teaching values through basketball. *Strategies* 5:5–8.

Hellison, D., and L. McBride. 1986. A responsibility curriculum for teaching health and physical education. *Oregon Journal of Health, Physical Education, Recreation, and Dance* 20:16–17.

Hellison, D., and T.J. Templin. 1991. *A reflective approach to teaching physical education.* Champaign, IL: Human Kinetics.

Hellison, D., and D. Walsh. 2002. Responsibility-based youth program evaluation: Investigating the investigations. *Quest* 54:292–307.

Hichwa, J. 1998. *Right fielders are people too.* Champaign, IL: Human Kinetics.

Hinson, C. 1997. *Games kids should play at recess.* 2nd ed. Wilmington, DE: PE Publishing.

Hinson, C. 2001. *Six steps to a trouble-free playground.* Wilmington, DE: PE Publishing.

Hodginson, H. 1991. Reform versus reality. *Phi Delta Kappan* 73:9–16.

Horrocks, R.N. 1977. Sportsmanship. *Journal of Physical Education, Recreation and Dance* 48:20–21.

Horrocks, R.N. 1978. Resolving conflict in the gymnasium. *Journal of Physical Education, Recreation and Dance* 49:61.

Howe, Q., Jr. 1991. *Under running laughter: Notes from a renegade classroom.* New York: Free Press.

Ianni, F.A.J. 1989. *The search for structure: A report on American youth today.* New York: Free Press.

Jones, R.S., and L.N. Tanner. 1981. Classroom discipline: The unclaimed legacy. *Phi Delta Kappan* 63:494–497.

Kamii, C., F.B. Clark, and A. Dominick. 1994. The six national goals: A road to disappointment. *Phi Delta Kappan* 75:672–677.

Keramidas, K. 1991. *Strategies to increase the individual motivation and cohesiveness of a junior male basketball team.* Master's thesis, University of Illinois at Chicago.

Kohn, A. 1993. Choices for children: Why and how to let students decide. *Phi Delta Kappan* 75:8–20.

Kunjufu, J. 1989. *Critical issues in educating African American youth.* Chicago: African American Images.

Lambert, L., and P. Grube. 1988. The physical/motor fitness learning center: A university-school collaborative effort. *Journal of Physical Education, Recreation and Dance* 59:70–73.

Lawson, H.A. 1984. Problem-setting for physical education and sport. *Quest* 36:48–60.

Lickona, T. 1991. *Educating for character: How our schools can teach respect and responsibility.* New York: Bantam.

Lickona, T. No date. *Eighteen strategies for helping kids take responsibility for building their own character.* Unpublished manuscript.

Lyon, H.C., Jr. 1971. *Learning to feel: Feeling to learn.* Columbus, OH: Merrill.

Maddi, S.R., S.C. Kobasa, and M. Hoover. 1979. An alienation test. *Journal of Humanistic Psychology* 19:73–76.

Martinek, T., and J.B. Griffith. 1993. Working with the learned helpless child. *Journal of Physical Education, Recreation and Dance* 64:17–20.

Martinek, T., and T. Schilling. 2002. *Developing compassionate leadership in underserved youth.* Unpublished paper.

Masser, L. 1990. Teaching for affective learning in elementary physical education. *Journal of Physical Education, Recreation and Dance* 61:18–19.

McCaslin, M., and T.L. Good. 1992. Compliant cognition: The misalignment of management and instruction goals in current school reform. *Educational Researcher* 21:4–17.

McDonald, J.P. 1992. *Teaching: Making sense of an uncertain craft.* New York: Teachers College Press.

McLaughlin, M.W., and S.J. Heath. 1993. Casting the self: Frames for identity and dilemmas for policy. In *Identity and inner city youth: Beyond ethnicity and gender,* ed. S.J. Heath and M.W. McLaughlin, 210–239. New York: Teachers College Press.

Meadows, B.J. 1992. Nurturing cooperation and responsibility in a school community. *Phi Delta Kappan* 73:480–481.

Mesa, P. 1992, November. *Keynote address.* First Annual At-Risk Youth Conference, Lake Tahoe, NV.

Mosston, M., and S. Ashworth. 1994. *Teaching physical education.* 4th ed. New York: Macmillan.

Mrugala, J. 2002. *Exploratory study of responsibility model practitioners.* Doctoral dissertation, University of Illinois at Chicago.

Murray, C.H., S.N. Smith, and E.H. West. 1989. Comparative personality development in adolescents: A critique. In *Black adolescents,* ed. R.L. Jones, 49–77. Berkeley, CA: Cobb & Henry.

Nicholls, J.G. 1989. *The competitive ethos and democratic education.* Cambridge, MA: Harvard University Press.

Nicholls, J.G., and S.P. Hazzard. 1993. *Education as adventure: Lessons from the second grade.* New York: Teachers College Press.

Noddings, N. 1992. *The challenge to care in schools.* New York: Teachers College Press.

Norton, D.L. 1976. *Personal destinies: A philosophy of ethical individualism.* Princeton, NJ: Princeton University Press.

Orlick, T. 1978. *The cooperation book of games and sports.* New York: Pantheon.

Orlick, T. 1980. *In pursuit of excellence.* Champaign, IL: Human Kinetics.

Parker, M., and D. Hellison. 2001. Teaching responsibility in physical education: Standards, outcomes, and beyond. *Journal of Physical Education, Recreation and Dance* 72:26–36.

Pastor, P. 2002. School discipline and the character of our schools. *Phi Delta Kappan* 83:658–661.

Petracek, R. 1998. *Strength building log.* Unpublished paper.

Power, F.C. 2002. Building democratic community: A radical approach to moral education. In *Bringing in a new era in character education,* ed. W. Damon, 129–148. Palo Alto, CA: Hoover Institution Press.

Prather, H. 1970. *Notes to myself. My struggle to become a person.* Moab, UT: Real Person Press.

Prather, H. 1972. *I touch the earth, the earth touches me.* New York: Doubleday.

Puka, B. 1987. Moral development without the philosophical captivation. *Moral Education Forum* 12:4–20.

Raffini, J.P. 1980. *Discipline: Negotiating conflicts with today's kids.* Englewood Cliffs, NJ: Prentice-Hall.

Ralph, J. 1989. Improving education for the disadvantaged: Do we know whom to help? *Phi Delta Kappan* 70:395–401.

Raths, L.E., M. Harmin, and S.B. Simon. 1966. *Values and teaching.* Columbus, OH: Merrill.

Richards, A. 1982. Seeking roots from Hahn. *Journal for Experiential Education* 5:22–25.

Romance, T.J., M.R. Weiss, and J. Bokoven. 1986. A program to promote moral development through elementary physical education. *Journal of Teaching in Physical Education* 5:126–136.

Romig, J. 1993. Two views backward [Book review]. *Journal of Teacher Education* 44:312–316.

Rubin, L. 1985. *Artistry in teaching*. New York: Random House.

Schafer, W. 1992. *Stress management for wellness*. 2nd ed. Fort Worth, TX: Harcourt Brace Jovanovich.

Schilling, T., T. Martinek, and C. Tan. 2001. Fostering youth development through empowerment. In *Sport in the twenty-first century: Alternatives for the new millennium*, ed. B.J. Lombardo, T.J. Caravella-Nadeau, H.S. Castagno, and V.H. Mancini, 169–179. Boston: Pearson.

Schlosser, L.K. 1992. Teacher distance and student disengagement: School lives on the margin. *Journal of Teacher Education* 43:128–140.

Schon, D.A. 1987. *Educating the reflective practitioner*. San Francisco: Jossey-Bass.

Shields, D.L.L., and B.J.L. Bredemeier. 1995. *Character development and physical activity*. Champaign, IL: Human Kinetics.

Siedentop, D. 1980. *Physical education: Introductory analysis*. 2nd ed. Dubuque, IA: Brown.

Siedentop, D. 1991. *Developing teaching skills in physical education*. 3rd ed. Mountain View, CA: Mayfield.

Siedentop, D. 1992. Thinking differently about secondary physical education. *Journal of Physical Education, Recreation and Dance* 63:69–72, 77.

Siedentop, D. 1994. *Sport education: Quality PE through positive sport experiences*. Champaign, IL: Human Kinetics.

Sizer, T.R. 1992. *Horace's school: Redesigning the American high school*. Boston: Houghton Mifflin.

Smith, M. 1990. Enhancing self-responsibility through a humanistic school program. *Journal of Physical Education, Recreation and Dance* 63:14–18.

Tappan, M.B. 1992. Educating for character: How our schools can teach respect and responsibility [Book review]. *Journal of Teacher Education* 43:386–389.

Thomas, C.E. 1983. *Sport in a philosophic context*. Philadelphia: Lea & Febiger.

Tom, A.R. 1984. *Teaching as a moral craft*. New York: Longman.

Trulson, M.E. 1986. Martial arts training as a "cure" for juvenile delinquency. *Human Relations* 39:1131–1140.

Veal, M.L., C.D. Ennis, D. Hellison, T. Martinek, and M. O'Sullivan. 2002. *Physical activity in high schools: Building models of caring*. Presentation at the American Alliance of Health, Physical Education, Recreation and Dance National Convention, San Diego.

Walberg, H.J., O. Reyes, and R.P. Weissberg. 1997. *Children and youth: Interdisciplinary perspectives*. Thousand Oaks, CA: Sage.

Walsh, D.S. 2002. Emerging strategies in the search for effective university-community collaborations. *Journal of Physical Education, Recreation and Dance* 73:50–53.

Weinberg, R.S., and D. Gould. 1999. *Foundations of sport and exercise psychology*. 2nd ed. Champaign, IL: Human Kinetics.

Weiner, L. 1993. *Preparing teachers for urban schools: Lessons from thirty years of school reform*. New York: Teachers College Press.

Williamson, K.M., and N. Georgiadis. 1992. Teaching an inner-city after-school program. *Journal of Physical Education, Recreation and Dance* 63:14–18.

Willis, J.D., and L.F. Campbell. 1992. *Exercise psychology*. Champaign, IL: Human Kinetics.

Zavacky, F. 1997. Motivating the I. *Teaching Elementary Physical Education* 8:30–31.

Index

About the Author

Don Hellison, PhD, is a professor in the College of Education and the Jane Addams College of Social Work at the University of Illinois at Chicago. He is best known for his work with at-risk youth and for the development of effective approaches to teaching physical activities in schools and social agencies. Since 1970 Hellison also has taught physical education part-time to young people in inner-city schools and community youth organizations, alternative schools, residential homes, and detention centers.

Hellison's ideas and experiences appear in a variety of journals and books, including *A Reflective Approach to Teaching Physical Education, Goals and Strategies for Teaching Physical Education, Youth Development and Physical Activity: Linking Universities and Communities,* and *Beyond Balls and Bats. Alienated Youth in the Gym.* He served as editor of *Quest* from 1996 to 1998.

He is a recipient of the Curriculum and Instruction Academy Scholar Award (2000), American Alliance for Health, Physical Education, Recreation and Dance (AAHPERD) Presidential Citation (2000), the National Association for Sport and Physical Education (NASPE) Hall of Fame Award (1999), National Association of Physical Education in Higher Education (NAPEHE) Scholar Award (1998), and the International Olympic Committee President's Prize (1995). Hellison is a member of AAHPERD, NASPE, and NAPEHE.